THE GOLD

AMSTERDAM

BONECHI

Distributor

NILSSON & LAMM B.V.
Pampuslaan 212 - 214
Postbus 195
1380 AD WEESP (Holland)

E-mail: Geotoer@nilsson-lamm.nl
Telefoon 0294 494949
Telefax 0294 494455

Project and editorial conception: Casa Editrice Bonechi
Publication Manager: Serena de Leonardis
Photo research, graphic design, layout, make-up and editing:
staff of the Casa Editrice Bonechi
Cover: Laura Settesoldi
Drawings and map p.102: Stefano Benini
Map of the city: Casa Editrice Bonechi

© Copyright by Casa Editrice Bonechi - Florence - Italy
E-mail: bonechi@bonechi.it - Internet: www.bonechi.it www.bonechi.com

Printed in Italy by Centro Stampa Editoriale Bonechi.

The photographs are property of the Casa Editrice Bonechi archives
with the exception of the following: page 10 (Lemcke), courtesy of the
Nederlands Bureau voor Toerisme; page 82, centre, and pages 92-93, courtesy of
Rijksmuseum Stichting; page 82 top left, and pages 95-97, courtesy of
Photo Service - Gruppo Editoriale Fabbri.

ISBN 88-476-0954-2

History

"Not a single Roman ruin, no trace of Charlemagne, not even a Romanesque church or cathedral" Nothing, in other words. The introduction to a famous book on Amsterdam leaves no doubt whatsoever: of the European cities, Amsterdam is the most recent and the most lacking in an ancient past and distant patrimonies. It is quite understandable: in 1975 this city celebrated its seventh centenary.

No traces were left by the Batavians, who sailed up the Rhine to land at the mouth of the Amstel. The Romans did not pay much attention to these unhealthy, marshy lands subject to dangerous flooding. And not even the Holy Roman Empire or Charlemagne managed to establish longlasting control over these foggy coasts. The Netherlands remained divided in small domains owned by feudal lords, counts, dukes and bishops. Yet maybe this historical gap was Amsterdam's fortune, enabling this future commercial capital of the Western world to expand freely without being restricted or conditioned, modelled by intelligent, open-minded town-planners who acted on behalf of a cultured, refined middle class. Unlike most European cities, Amsterdam is not the result of the wordly ambitions of a sovereign or emperor, but it is a city built entirely by rich traders and lovers of beauty.

The original centre of Amsterdam was created in about 1200 when the Waterlanders from the North moved to the mouth of the Amstel in search of more secure, fertile land. They built a small fishing village around a castle erected on a dyke – dam in Dutch – which, separating the Amstel from the IJ, a wide arm of the Zuidersee, protected their huts from flooding. The dyke stood on the very spot where the Royal Palace was to be built centuries later.

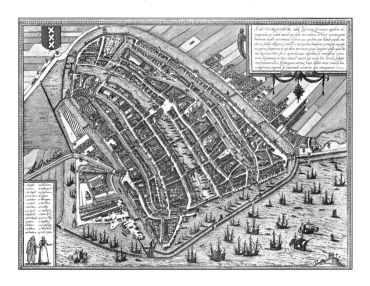

It was Floris V, one of the numerous local lords, who noticed the village unimaginatively named Amstelledamme, or dyke on the Amstel, by its inhabitants. The count granted the village exemption from customs duties to establish free trade. Never was a decree so well-timed; unwittingly, Floris V was the initiator of the trading fortunes of the future city of Amsterdam. The business acumen of the fishermen saw to the rest. They improved their seafaring ability and travelled the oceans, going as far as Portugal to buy salt and crossing the Baltic for timber. They did not lack inventiveness, like unknown Beukels who discovered a way to preserve herrings, which greatly increased his earnings. Amsterdam also grew internationally; it adhered to the Hanseatic League in 1358 and then to the Cologne League in 1367, becoming a hub.

It was also lucky enough to be the scene of a miracle in 1345. A consecrated host that refused to burn when it was thrown into the fire is "the miracle of Amsterdam"; in short, the little town became the destination of non-stop pilgrimages. The small chapel on Kalverstraat where the miracle is said to have taken place was also visited by Emperor Maximilian I who, to express his gratitude, granted Amsterdam the right to use his imperial crown in its coat-of-arms.

Luck, skill and tenacity, apart from a capacity to react to disasters such as the fires of 1421 and 1452 which razed the town to the ground, are the ingredients which enabled Amsterdam to count 30.000 inhabitants in 1551. The signs of the great Golden Century could already be glimpsed.

Amsterdam was very jealous of its autonomy and liberality; in fact, during the Spanish occupation, it became the refuge for all nationalities of victims of persecution: Portuguese Jews, Jews fleeing from the massacre of Antwerp, French Huguenots and English Dissenters. In this way, new intellectual classes and highly skilled craftsmen such as the Antwerp diamond cutters settled there.

These were troubled times for Europe. During the 16th century, the religious wars between the Catholic inquisitors and Supporters of the Reform broke out. Holland like other European countries was a battleground: in 1567 the Spanish sent the fierce Duke of Alba to rout the Protestants. The terror of the Inquisition was opposed by the Oranges with William the Taciturn, founder of the dynasty that still governs The Netherlands today. During the war of independence against Spain, Amsterdam changed sides. Taking the part of the occupiers, the town surrendered to the Oranges and proclaimed itself in favour of the war against the Spanish dominators. This was in 1578: the old governors of the town, faithful to the Spanish sovereigns, were chased away and Amsterdam was governed by a new ruling class: immigrants, Protestants, supporters of the Reform and merchants who gave life to the "Alteratie", a radical change in the life of the town. One year later in 1579, the seven Protestant provinces north of the Rhine signed the peace treaty of Utrecht and Amsterdam could return with new enthusiasm to its trade. Merchants rose to power once and for all and modelled the heights of glory of a town destined to become a world power. For Amsterdam navigators, the earth knew no bounds; this was at the time of the rich tea, coffee, tobacco, cocoa, rubber, spices and diamonds trades. Great financial concentrations such as the Bank of Amsterdam (1608) were set up and powerful trading companies such as the feared VOC, the East Indes Company (1612), were founded followed by the Company of the North (1614), the Near East (1614) and above all by the Company of the West Indes (1621). Colonies were established in Brazil between 1624 and 1654 and especially in the Eastern countries, and monopolies were set up; it is to be remembered that the VOC became the strongest trading organisation in the world. No less than 150 vessels sailed the oceans under its flag, escorted by 40 warships and defended by an army of ten thousand men. On the other side of the world, Henry Hudson was sent in search of a passage to China, doubling the American continent. The navigator was unsuccessful in his undertaking, but he explored a large bay, discovered Manhattan island and decided that it was a suitable place to found Nieuw Amsterdam, which was later to be called New York. The Dutch had no limits: they were the first white men to disembark in Australia and discovered Tasmania, New Zealand and the Fiji Islands. Amsterdam traders were the only ones to deal with Japan even during the 200 years of absolute isolation of that very distant archipelago.

Amsterdam was the leading port in the world: the city expanded beyond the inner walls and town-planners built the Herengracht, Keizergracht and Prinsengracht. Amsterdam was the city of great artists such as Rembrandt and Vermeer and applied sciences underwent great developments: Van Leeuwenhoek invented the microscope, Boerhaave's lectures on medicine attracted students from all over Europe, optics performed miracles and diamond cutters became world famous. This was during the 17th century, the Golden Century, a hitherto unseen and unequalled splendour. The city competed openly, also on a military scale, with the greatest sea power at the time: England. It was a spectacular period but the challenge against the English proved to be too demanding for Amsterdam. The Dutch helped American rebels in their struggle against England and the English did not hesitate to take revenge. In fact, 1780 marked the beginning of the fall of the star of Amsterdam. Napoleon's armies were hell bent on the conquest of Europe and did not spare Holland: Napoleon invaded The Netherlands, defeated the Batavian Republic, created by the streams of the French Revolution and appointed his brother, Louis Bonaparte, King of Holland.

A short-lived reign: in 1813 Napoleon's star had already set. Louis Bonaparte was removed from power and the Oranges returned to the throne with William I. These were the bases for the Holland of today: no longer the glory of the great sea *power, no longer the proud eruptions of the Golden Century, but a daily struggle to resconstruct şolid wealth. It was a question of pondering over a city, restoring its crumbling ghettos and protecting the land from the sea. Holland gradually emerged from its great seafaring history and asserted its neutrality. It did not get involved in the First World War, but it suffered the consequences: economic depression, lack of fuel and food. During the years that followed immediately after the Second World War, sensational success against the sea was recorded: the Dutch managed to reclaim land from the North Sea and the Zuidersee was transformed into a large lake with the construction of the Afsluitdijk, a thirty kilometer long dyke between Friesland and the Province of North Holland. Holland was overcome by the Nazi fury and in 1940 Hitler's armies occupied Amsterdam and started deporting Jews. The courageous dockers' strikes were of little avail and during the Nazi occupation 100,000 Dutch Jews died in German concentration camps. On the 5th May 1945, Canadian troops freed Amsterdam. Holland is no longer a great power, but a small state which has to build its future. It has an outstanding quality: tolerance. Amsterdam is one of the freest cities in the world. The provos movement started here in 1968 and in 1970, the Kabouters or Party of Gnomes elected five of their representatives to the town council. Thousands of young people chose Amsterdam as their European capital; they met on the steps of the National Monument on the Dam. During the years that followed, the public authorities made every effort to improve the city's structures and make the city itself an agreeable place to live in; in doing so they were given ample consensus. Hence, Amsterdam underwent the immense and important projects that were to change its appearance but which did not leave it disfigured in any particular way. Even though it has been and still is the object of criticism and controversy (and this is only natural) much of the work either already completed or still underway has involved reconstruction and improvement rather than actual demolition.*

Today, Amsterdam is ceaselessly developing. The air traffic going through Schiphol airport, which was renovated in 1993, is constantly increasing. Audacious skyscrapers recently erected in the southern part of the city can be seen stretching upwards to the East and the West, while the eastern part of the port (the fifth largest in Europe) has become one of the most exclusive residential areas in Amsterdam after the transformation of what were previously factories. There are many projects still underway, both in this area and to the West of the city. And at long last the subway has been completed, thanks to the use of advanced technologies that allow tunnels to be drilled even in swampy areas like those found in Amsterdam. The line linking the North and South of the city should be finished within a few years.

Index of the Itineraries

Dam • National Monument • Royal Palace •
Madame Tussaud Scenerama • Nieuwe Kerk •
Westerkerk • Anne Frank House • The Jordaan •
Noorderkerk • Ronde Lutherse Kerk

Anne Frank House
•p. 20

Westerkerk
•p. 19

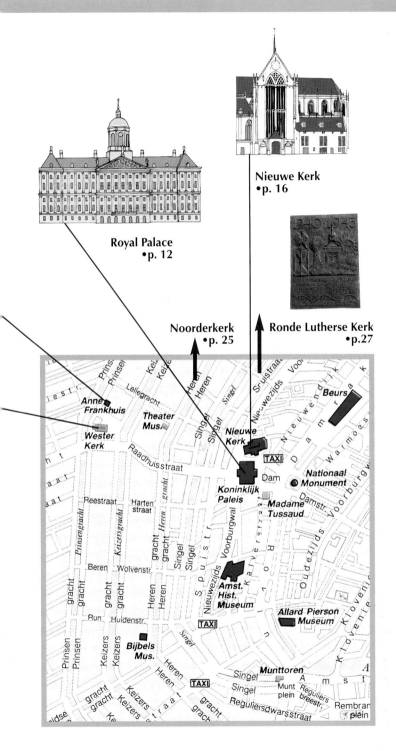

Royal Palace
•p. 12

Nieuwe Kerk
•p. 16

Noorderkerk
•p. 25

Ronde Lutherse Kerk
•p.27

9

THE DAM

It is the most famous square in Holland. The fishing village which was later transformed into Amsterdam was built right on this very spot in about 1270. It is the ideal city centre, even if it ceased to be the geographic heart and administrative seat years ago. Right throughout the sixties, hippies and provos from all over Europe met at the Dam. Only during the day does the square continue to teem with young people and visitors from all over the world. They sit on the white steps of the National Monument, a favourite, historic meeting place.

DAM
CENTRUM

It is the Dam that gave the city its name. In this square the Waterlanders, who originally lived in the North on the sea, built the dam, blocking the flow of the Amstel and separating it from the IJ, a wide arm of the Zuidersee. The Waterlanders were looking for rich, fertile land to serve also as a barrier. They landed on the sandy banks of the mouth of the Amstel, and to protect themselves against the tides and recurring flooding on the river, they built this initial dyke which constituted their quick fortune. In short, the Dam became the space in which the entire community met for official ceremonies and the most important events, a deeprooted habit still maintained by Amsterdam's citizens. In the Middle Ages the Dam faced the sea, from where ships set sail for the North Sea. Today the end part of the Amstel has completely disappeared, its flow having been deviated: its mouth has been silted up between the Damrak and Rokin, the two main channels of communication which cross the Dam, cutting it in half.

An aerial view of Dam square.

National monument – The Dam is the traditional starting point for all sightseeing tours of Amsterdam. A white obelisk rises up in the centre of the square. It is the Dutch national monument built after the Second World War to commemorate its victims. It was designed by J. P. Oud and decorated with *sculptures* by J. W. Raedecker. The four male figures recall the tragedies of war, the woman and child symbolize peace while the men with dogs portray resistance to the invaders. At the back of the obelisk are *twelve urns*: eleven contain a fistful of earth from each Dutch province, whereas the twelfth is earth of Indonesia, the last ex-colony of the vast Dutch empire. In 1956 Queen Juliana dedicated the monument to the All Souls' Day, the 4th May, a public holiday; and every year Dutch kings or queens pay honour to war victims at the Dam.

At eight o'clock in the evening of the same day, the whole country comes to a standstill for two minutes' silence.

The Dam is the only square in Amsterdam where there are evident traces of pomp and ceremony: in fact, it is the only square in town with royal pretensions.

The national monument in memory of those who lost their lives in the Second World War.

11

The Wild Man's House.

Behind the obelisk, the Grand Hotel Krasnapolski faces the **Wild Man's House** with "De Gekroonde Wildeman", one of Amsterdam's oldest taverns (1689).

THE ROYAL PALACE

In front of the national monument, the imposing neoclassical façade of the Koninklijk Paleis or Royal Palace, which is open from mid-June to mid-September, dominates the Dam. It does not look like a palace of Amsterdam and betrays the intention of the city's authorities to build a town hall in keeping with the prestige and power of Europe's commercial capital during the 17th century. It is attributed to the architect, Jacob van Campen, who faithfully followed the classic architectural themes of ancient Rome in 1640. Only eight years later, once the victorious war against Spain was over, it was decided to commence the building of Van Campen's project. On the 28th October 1648, the first stone was laid. Ten months beforehand the 13,659 piles supporting the entire palace were set in the marshy ground. 1655 marked the inauguration of the first wing of the future town hall of Amsterdam which was completed seven years later by another architect, Daniël Stalpaert. The palace on the Dam was at the time the largest, most expensive townhall in Europe. A Dutch poet, Costan-

The Royal Palace.

tijn Huygens, went as far as defining it the eighth wonder of the world. Another poet, the greatest Dutch poet, Joost van den Vondel, dedicated a poem of 1378 verses to it. The sculptor Artus Quellijn and two pupils of Rembrandt, Ferdinand Bol and Govert Flinck, the very best the Dutch Golden Century could offer, contributed to the pomp of the palace.

For over a century the palace was the city's seat of government. Only in 1808, when Louis Bonaparte, Napoleon's brother, crowned himself King of The

Allegorical sculptures by Artus Quellijn on the façade of the Royal Palace.

Royal Palace – The Citizens' Hall.

Netherlands was the palace transformed into a royal residence. It was a short-lived reign: Bonaparte was forced to leave a matter of two years later and he left behind in the halls of the palace one of the most complete collections of Empire style furniture in the world.

After Bonaparte's abdication, William I, the new King of The Netherlands gave the palace back to the city, but the government of Amsterdam could not cover the huge cost of upkeep of the building. William remained there as a temporary guest. In 1936 the Royal Palace became State property and the royal family uses it only for official ceremonies, preferring the Huis ten Bosch residence in the outskirts of The Hague.

Interior – The palace reflects the commercial pride of the Golden Century: the **Citizens' Hall**, one of the most magnificent halls of government in Europe, is the heart of the building. The *Virgin of Amsterdam* towers over an authentic planisphere. Sculptured in marble are the lands that Dutch traders covered tirelessly in perennial search of new trade. In this immense hall, the present Queen of The Netherlands, Beatrix, and Claus von Amsberg celebrated their wedding in 1966.

In the **Minor Affairs of State Hall**, the *statue of Apollo,* god of the sun and music, urges a peaceful solution to all dissension, while the severe bas-reliefs of the *Pietà, Wisdom and Justice* warn visitors of the **Judgement Hall**, room in which judges used to meet to pronounce death sentences.

Behind the Royal Palace, at Nieuwezijds Voorburgwal no.182, there is a rather bizarre Dutch Renaissance style building, designed by C.P. Peters at the end of the 19th century and the cause of much debate. For some time it was the General Post Office, then in 1990 it was converted into the **Magna Plaza** shopping mall.

The Postkantoor, the former General Post Office building that now houses the Magna Plaza.

MADAME TUSSAUD SCENERAMA

This waxworks museum is above the Peek & Cloppenburg department store in Dam Square, about ten minutes walking distance from the central railway station. It is one of the many museums spread all over the world that bear the name of the French sculptress who specialised in making wax models of the heads of famous people guillotined during the French Revolution.

Madame Tussaud opened her first museum in London in 1836 and to this day the wax models are still made in the London workshops and according to her methods.

Before a model is made, hundreds of photographs are taken of the subject as well as all the measurements then, when it is finished, a wig of real hair is applied to the head. Present-day celebrities immortalised in wax sometimes donate articles of clothing and accessories from their personal wardrobes.

Thanks to the audio-animatronic system fitted in the Madame Tussaud museum in Amsterdam, visitors can watch scenes depicting daily life during the Golden Century in Holland, or even see Rembrandt himself busily painting away at his easel. A 'live' representation of a Vermeer painting, or a sudden face-to-face encounter with a famous politician or film actor, still alive or from the past, can make the visit even more amusing.

Children love the Scenerama attractions, though some of the scenes might frighten the smaller ones.

There is a beautiful view of the Dam from the window on the fourth floor.

NIEUWE KERK

Alongside the Royal Palace, the New Church, Nieuwe Kerk, occupies a corner of the Dam. The construction of this basilica commenced in about 1400 in the fruit orchard of the house of Willem Eggert, a rich banker and treasurer of count William VI of Holland. The foundation deed of the Nieuwe Kerk was initialled in 1408 by the bishop of Utrecht, Frederick. His signature sanctioned the division of Amsterdam into two parishes: the old diocese of the Oude Kerk, could no longer attend to a city in continuous expansion. Unwittingly, with his decision, Frederick initiated the centuries-old rivalry between the two churches. It was to be an endless challenge and pursuit of embellishment, novelty and magnificence even if the Nieuwe Kerk never managed to have the highest belltower in the city for financial reasons. In 1321 and 1452 the Nieuwe Kerk was badly damaged by fires which threatened to destroy Amsterdam. Restoration works were immediately carried out and after the second fire, the church took on its final late Gothic structure.

Another fire, due to an artisan's being distracted, devastated the church in 1645 and Jacob van Campen had to guide new restoration, leaving a Renaissance stamp on the Nieuwe Kerk which was reconsecrated in time to celebrate thanksgiving rites for the peace of Munster.

Today the Nieuwe Kerk is a covered extension of the Dam; conferences, exhibitions and debates are held in its interior as in all Protestant churches. Even a café, "t nieuwe café," occupies a corner of the church and opens onto the square.

Interior – It is lit by the light that penetrates from 75 windows, only one of which still has its original stained-glass depicting the handing over of the city's weapons to its magistrates. But the real jewel of the church is the *pulpit,* a baroque masterpiece by Albert Vinckenbrinck and his pupils, and the *organ,* designed by Van Campen. The inlay work around the pulpit kept Vinckenbrinck busy for 13 years: the figures of the four evangelists are surrounded by images of Hope, Charity, Faith, Justice, Prudence and Strength.

Two views of the Nieuwe Kerk.

Nieuwe Kerk – two views of the interior; the enormous
organ was designed by Jacob van Campen.

The Nieuwe Kerk is the burial place of numerous famous Dutchmen: naval heroes such as admiral De Ruyter, who died from
wounds he received at the battle of Messina (1676) against the
French fleet deserved sumptuous mausoleums, while the greatest
Dutch poet, Joost van den Vondel, is buried under a more modest
monument.

The Kings of and Queens of The Netherlands are crowned
in the Nieuwe Kerk, starting with William I in 1814.
Princess Juliana was crowned on the 6th September
1948, whereas her daughter Beatrix was crowned on the
30th April 1980, in a Nieuwe Kerk renewed after 22
years of careful restoration.

Going around the back, the Nieuwe Kerk penetrates into a narrow,
splendid street: the **Gravenstraat**. It is a street of small, exclusive
shops, each with its own glori-
ous past. **No. 18** is the site of
"De Drie Flesjes," The Three Little Bottles, a famous tasting
house where one can taste the
jenever (the famous Dutch gin)
in a stupendous 17th century
interior. At **no. 28** is the "Fro-
magerie Crignon", a tiny restaurant whose cuisine is based entirely on cheese.

Westerkerk, the church that boasts the highest bell-tower in Amsterdam.

Having crossed the very busy Nieuwezijds Voorburgwal, meaning the walls of the new district which were once the city's primitive boundary, one runs into Raadhuisstraat, a thoroughfare that cuts across the entire canal network taking you in a matter of five minutes to the western boundary of the historic centre, the **Prinsengracht** in line with the **Westermarkt**. **No. 6** of this beautiful square was the residence of Descartes, one of the most fertile thinkers who left his critical mark on Amsterdam when he stated that in this city of traders "everybody, except for me, does business and only thinks of his earnings. I could live here forever without anybody being aware of my existence".

WESTERKERK

An 85-metre high bell-tower, the highest in town and nicknamed Langer Jan, is the consecrated symbol of Amsterdam and of the Westerkerk, the Western Church, by Hendrick de Keyser, a famous name in Dutch architecture. After the victory of Protestantism, as part of an ambitious project to enlarge the town, De Keyser started the construction of a Renaissance church with unusual Gothic details in 1619. De Keyser never lived to see his work completed; it was his son Pieter and Cornelius Dancker who completed the church and built the tower that was crowned by a sphere with the imperial crown of Maximilian I of Austria.
Careful restoration works, carried out in 1985-90, brought up to light the splendid original colours of the bricks and stones of the building.

Interior – The Westerkerk, which was consecrated during Pentecost in 1631, has a double cross plan divided by two rows of Tuscan style columns. The **nave** was covered with a barrel vault in wood because the marshy ground of the city did not allow the use of heavier materials.
A plate on a column of the north aisle serves as a reminder that Rembrandt was buried in the Westerkerk. The memorial tablet was fixed in place in 1906 during the third centenary of the famous artist's death, but, as a matter of fact, nobody knows exactly where he was buried and even the text of the tablet is reticent. In fact, it ignores the fact that Rembrandt was buried in the Westerkerk only because his family did not have enough money for a burial in keeping with the fame of a great artist.

The house at Westermarkt 6 where the philosopher Descartes lived.

The monument to homosexuals, designed by Karin Daan and set near the Westerkerk in 1986. It commemorates those who were persecuted during the Nazi regime for their sexuality.

19

Anne Frank house, visited by tourists from all over the world.

The entrance to
Anne Frank house.

ANNE FRANK HOUSE

To the left of the Westerkerk is a small statue. It portrays a little girl: Anne Frank. Her house is very near: at number 263 Prinsengracht, a place of pilgrimage for thousands of people.

Anne Frank house-museum is convincing, lasting evidence and a constant accusation of Naziism. In this house Anne Frank hid with her parents, her sister Margot, the Van Pels family and Mr. Pfeffer for over two years, from July 1942 to August 1944. Anne Frank house is like thousands of others in the old part of Amsterdam. It was built in 1653 by a trader. Steep, narrow stairs, use made of upper spaces in two houses, one on top of the other and separated by a courtyard. The cost of houses in Amsterdam was established according to their width and the portion they occupied on the pavements and on the quays of canals. This is why the house of Anne Frank, like all the houses in the city, developed in a vertical and not in a horizontal direction.

In 1940, Otto Frank, Anne's father, installed his wholesale spice trading company on the

Prinsengracht. The Frank family had fled from Frankfurt in Germany after the coming of Naziism. Otto Frank immediately understood the consequences of the German invasion of The Netherlands and started turning the back part of their house into a hiding-place. Helped by some of the company employees, the Franks and their friends disappeared in July 1942. Two floors with tiny rooms and an attic concealed by a revolving library were the refuge of this small group of Jews.

Anne started writing her famous diary in 1940. She had been given it for her thirteenth birthday; everyday she made a note of the desperate joys, anxieties and hopes of that handful of people who watched the approach of the allied troops who had landed in Normandy. Koophuis and Kraler, employes of the Franks, and two typists, Miep and Elly, managed to procure food, clothes and books for the Franks.

" Our secret abode has now become an actual hideaway."

21st August 1942

Anne wrote the last page of her diary on the 1st August 1944. On the 4th the two Jewish families were betrayed to the Gestapo and arrested. Anne Frank's diary was salvaged; a German policeman turned her papers upside down on the floor and left them there. The Franks were deported to Germany and ended up at Auschwitz. Almost all of them died: the mother of hardship, Hermann van Pels in a gas chamber, Fritz Pfeffer at Neuengamme while Anne and Margot died of typhus fever two months before the end of the war at Bergen Belsen. Only Otto Frank was saved when the Russians freed Auschwitz. The old typist, Miep, managed to gather together the sheets of Anne's diary and handed them to her father when he returned to Amsterdam. With the advice of friends, Otto Frank decided to publish his daughter's testimony in 1947: *Het Achterhuis* shook world opinion. It was translated into fifty languages and over 13 million copies were sold. In 1957 the house of Anne Frank risked being demolished. Some of Amsterdam's inhabitants opposed this and formed the Anne Frank Foundation, transforming her house into a museum. But the building on the Prinsengracht is much more than a simple museum: on the first floor of her house are collected and updated accurate evidence and documents on new forms of social discrimination, and antisemitism.

Anne Frankhuis

THE JORDAAN

This is the most beautiful part of Amsterdam. And curiously contradictory, too: when the Jordaan was built it was an overpopulated neighbourhood, a mass of hovels piled one on top of the other. Impoverished craftsmen inhabited the area and the contrast that reigned between the shacks that huddled together in the Jordaan and the splendid Baroque dwellings on the banks of the nearby canals was unpleasantly conspicuous. So much so that two churches had to be built very near each other, the Westerkerk and the Noorderkerk, so that the middle classes living in Prinsengracht and the poor of the Jordaan area were not forced to worship in the same church. The Jordaan became the district for the desperate, the only place where those fleeing from all sorts of persecution could find shelter. The French Huguenots, escaping from their country after Louis XIV abolished the Edict of Nantes in 1685, lived here for many years.

These sad, legendary origins were followed by a present of bohémien glory: the Jordaan is a fashionable district, a favourite haunt of artists, young people and intellectuals. It is Amsterdam's "village", which has grown proud of its original history.

In the Jordaan, one lives outdoors; originally one was forced to do so by sheer necessity. Houses were small, crowded and impossible to live in. Inhabitants found refuge and tranquillity on the streets, among the canals and in the numerous pubs and taverns. Nowadays in the Jordaan, one still lives outdoors: its atmosphere is contagious, cheerful and convivial. The Jordaan is full of small shops, boutiques, artisan workshops and, above all, Amsterdam's best *bruine cafés*, the famous cafés blackened by smoke. During the month of September the streets of the Jordaan, as if in a final burst of summer, go mad with the district's festival. The festival lasts ten days with all the streets lit up, outdoor dinners, receptions, dances, exhi-

Houses along the Egelantiersgracht.

bitions, processions and a tug-of-war between the two banks of a canal.

Many have tried to explain the name Jordaan: the most reliable thesis is that it derives from the French word "jardin" meaning garden. It is a rather strained interpretation which is justified by the fact that the Jordaaners managed to attend to small gardens and vegetable patches around their houses despite their poverty. Furthermore, all the streets of the district and all the canals have floreal names: Lindenstraat, Rozengracht, Bloemgracht, etc.

Furthermore, there are no great monuments in the Jordaan. The Baroque wealth of the "other" Amsterdam is far removed but do not be deceived: out of 8,000 houses in the Jordaan, at least 800 have been declared national monuments. This is why one must stroll through this district, considered to be the most beautiful in Amsterdam, with its hidden charm.

From the Westermarkt, a bridge over the Prinsengracht leads to the **Rozengracht**, the "street of roses" that cuts the island of the Jordaan in two. It is the only busy street in the district and the only thoroughfare for those wishing to reach the centre of Amsterdam from the western part of the city. It can be avoided, even though it must be remembered that Rembrandt moved here after falling out of favour and later died here; in fact **no. 184** is marked by a

The Keijzer Koffie en Thee, the beautiful old coffee and spice shop on Prinsengracht.

commemorative plate. After the bridge, turn immediately right into Prinsengracht in line with a beautiful shop at **no. 180** selling coffee and spices: the "Keijzer Koffie en Thee," founded here in 1839. A few yards further on to the left is a transversal canal, the **Bloemgracht**, once known as the Jordaan's "Gentlemen's canal". This was the residential area of the richest craftsmen and therefore contains the most beautiful houses. The traces of this relative prosperity are still evident and this magnificent canal offers many points of interest: The Bloemgracht houses are also worth looking at: at **no. 98** the unadorned building of the Apostolic Mission, at **nos. 83-85** two twin gables, at nos. 87-91 three houses dated 1645. Now property of the Hendrick de Keyser Foundation, they are called the "**Three**

23

Bloemgracht – the Three Hendriks and (below) the house at no. 97.

Hendriks." At **no. 97** a charming home bearing the name of the owner inscribed in a plate situated above the entrance. In short, one has reached the western boundary of the Jordaan, Lijnbaansgracht. Turn right and you will find, after **Egelantiersgracht**, another delightful canal. It is worth mentioning the houses from **no. 215** to **201**, all in the same style; they belonged to the same family as can be seen from the coats-of-arms on the gable. Between **no. 139** and **107** you will find a charitable institution, **Sint Andrieshof**. Ask if you can enter: the inner courtyard is worth this act of bravery to be able to admire the architecture of these old almshouses. In the Jordaan, but also elsewhere, these charitable institutions abound. Between the 17th and 18th centuries they sprung up in tens. The founder was usually a rich trader willing to help the old and needy of his religious sect for all kinds of reasons. He would then build houses with very simple lines: a square courtyard, tiny residences to the sides and an entrance door which was almost invisible from the street. He then ceded it to the community which in turn undertook to respect the rules that he laid down. An administrator, whose home opened onto the courtyard supervised these communities. Here, having reached the point where Eerste Leliedwarsstraat crosses over, you can enjoy a good view of the bell-tower of the Westerkerk. At the bottom of Egelantiersgracht is to be found a small, famous café, "'t Smalle," an ideal example of a *bruine café* or café whose walls are blackened by clients' smoke. It was here that Peter Hoppe (famous in The Netherlands for his *jenever*, the typical Dutch gin) installed the first alembics of his spirits distillery

in 1780. At this point, one is once again on the Prinsengracht. Take a double turn left and one will run into **Egelantiersstraat**. At **no. 52** is an unconventional coat-of-arms: a writing hand. It commemorates the old owner of the house: a specialist in the art of writing.
Right nextdoor is the half-hidden entrance to the **Claes-Claeszhofje**, another old age home founded in 1626 by a Baptist fabrics merchant. Today it is a youth hostel mainly for students from the Academy of Music. It is worth visiting the three, narrow, inner courtyards. Turn right for Eerste Egelantiersdwarsstraat and then sharp left for Tuinstraat, meaning Garden Street. Beyond a small garden open to the public is another charitable institution, the **Regenboogsliefdehofje**.

The 't Smalle café.

One then reaches **Tweede Tuindwarsstraat**: one of the Jordaan's business streets, full of street cafés, little restaurants and shops of all kinds. Having reached Westerstraat and Tichelstraat, with the coat-of-arms of Batavia – the old name for Djakarta – displayed at **nos. 53** and **33**, bear right for Karthuizersstraat.

The Noorderkerk – the first church in the city built on a Greek cross plan.

Yet another charitable institution: the **Huiszitten-Weduwenhofje**. Originally built for widows, nowadays it lodges young people. This street finally leads into Lindenstraat which goes directly to **Noordermarkt**, the square of the Noorderkerk. Some of the coats-of-arms of the houses to the left are interesting: a sheep at **no. 19**, a hen at **no. 18** and a cow at **no. 17**.
Just in face stands the imposing **Noorderkerk** that was built in 1620 by Hendrick Staets and Hendrick de Keyser and was the first to break the architectural tradition of the nave, transept, chancel and altar. Instead, the Noorderkerk was built in a Greek cross plan: four

arms of equal length that meet in the middle. Noordermarkt faces Prinsengracht, one of the most charming sights in town. Following the canal, to the left, is the most famous café in the area, the **"Papeneiland"**; behind this pub decorated with ceramics is the beginning of **Lindengracht**, a lovely tree-lined avenue, animated every saturday by a lively market.

Coats-of-arms appear again on Lindengracht. At **no. 57** everything is upside down: the inscription "T' Hcargnednil" which is read back to front is the name of the street, the year and the

At the entrance to the Noorderkerk, the sculpted group statue called 'Unity means strength', commemorating the Jordaan revolt.

The Noorderkerk.

figure representing fish swimming peacefully on the leafy branch of a tree. At the beginning of the avenue stands the statue of a famous Dutch writer: Theo Thijssen who taught for many years at a school in the Jordaan. The long walk through the Jordaan ends by turning right again into **Driehoekstraat**, a strange triangular street that marks the northern boundary of the district. Return towards Papeneiland along **Brouwersgracht**, the canal which owes its name to old breweries built there. It is also the docking place for Amsterdam's most famous **house-boats**, embellished by hundreds of plants, flowers and decorations of all kinds and is also the canal which has kept its old warehouses to the right, with a pulley almost in line with the roof.

RONDE LUTHERSE KERK

The outstanding feature is without a shadow of doubt its copper **dome** 45-metres high. With its impressive quay, it reigns supreme over the low houses of what was the herring traders' district. It is a church famous for its figures: 2 million bricks to build it, 3615 piles and the copper which was given by Charles XI of Sweden. A fire destroyed it in 1882. It was then rebuilt, but its good fortune came to an end. The district was becoming depopulated and the Ronde Lutherse Kerk followed in the wake of its decadence. In 1935 it was deconsecrated and sealed. It was used as a deposit and warehouse until an American multinational company cast its eyes on its empty spaces. They were in the process of building a luxury hotel right alongside the church and proposed to restore it to adapt it for use as halls for congresses and conferences, banquets and plays. The proposal was accepted and the Ronde Lutherse Kerk is a centre for meetings and concerts nowadays.

Nieuwendijk is only a couple of paces away. At no. 16 of this noisy street is the **Dutch Arts and Crafts Centre**. At first sight, it appears to be a tourist trap; on the contrary it is an interesting, huge basement where you can discover and admire talented craftsmen at work on typical Dutch productions divided into small stands: diamond-cutters, glass-blowers, potters and printers, not to mention clog and copper-forging craftsmen.

The deconsecrated Ronde Lutherse Kerk, now a congress centre.

27

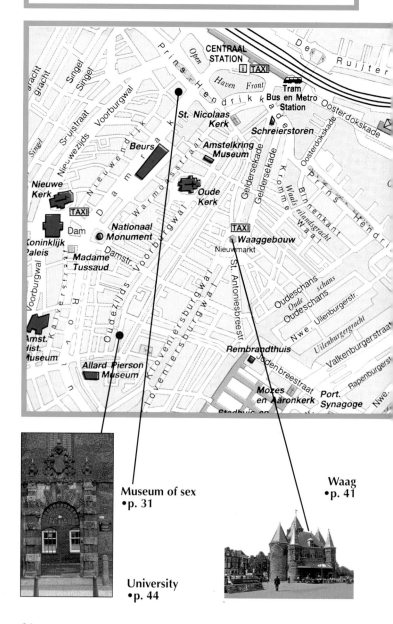

Museum of sex
•p. 31

University
•p. 44

Waag
•p. 41

Oude Kerk
•p. 33

Central Station
•p. 30

Damrak
•p. 31

CENTRAL STATION

LIt is not surprising that a station is a tourist attraction. Amsterdam station is in fact an authentic monument, a masterpiece by Pieter Cuypers, the architect who also designed the Rijksmuseum. It is therefore no surprise to find crowds of people looking up admiringly at this huge building, instead of only going there to catch a train. It was designed and built at the end of the 19th century and was erected on three artificial islands facing the port on 8687 piles. It is necessary to cross its immense halls to appreciate its beauty. The square in front of it is like an enormous parade ground which gives you a semicircular view of Amsterdam while the station interior is almost a cathedral with its nave and aisles. One can enter it to get to the back door, which looks directly onto the **IJ** the arm of sea that flows into the **IJsselmeer** and onto the **port** of Amsterdam. On looking to the left, a skyscraper is the port's tower: the **Havengebouw** (see page 122).

Central Station – the Gothic and Renaissance elements of its façade recall that of the Rijkmuseum. Above: one of the towers at the sides of the building, with a weather vane.

Set off along one of Amsterdam's main streets, right in front of the station: the **Damrak**, a large thoroughfare that leads directly to the Dam. It is a commercial road, full of shops, antique dealers' shops, boutiques and pubs. Points of interest: the **Museum of Sex** at no. 26 and a well stocked English bookshop, Allert de Lange, at no. 64.

A long red-brick building stands out to the left of the Damrak. It is a squat, imposing parallelepiped built between 1898 and 1903. It was one of Amsterdam's business centres: the **Stock Exchange**. It was built by Hendrick Petrus Berlage, pupil of Cuypers, and for its times it was listed among the ultramodern masterpieces of architecture. Nowadays the building houses the **Beurs van Berlage Museum**.

On reaching **Beursplein**, make a U-turn around the building and come back towards Damrak basin along the back of the Stock Exchange. At the bottom, turn right, crossing the imaginary boundary between the business part of Amsterdam, full of rich buyers, and the **Red-Light District**, *Walletjes,* meaning Little Walls, a triangle of very old, crumbling houses which has developed around the port and the oldest church in town, the **Oude Kerk** (see page 33). An area famous for its prostitutes on display behind glass windows, it is not recent history dating back as far as the 14th century.

Beurs van Berlage – the imposing red-brick building, named after the architect who designed it at the beginning of the 20th century, is considered a milestone in modern Dutch architecture.

The setting is almost romantic: the narrow streets, charming canals and the dilapidated façades of the **Oudezijds Voorburgwal** and the parallel **Oudezijds Achterburgwal** clash with the windows displaying prostitutes who offer themselves to spectators and clients.

Walletjes is a strange mixture of lovely, old shops run by old ladies, impeccable Protestant clergymen and sex-shops. One may find its grotesqueness either sad or amusing; it is a fact that everybody visits it and even the inhabitants of Amsterdam consider it a tourist attraction. It must be remembered that Amsterdam is the symbol of tolerance.

One of the points in which the contrast between the red lights and charm of Walletjes is most noticeable is **Oudekerksplein**. Once in **Warmoesstraat**, the narrowest of Amsterdam's old commercial streets and a compact row of bars and cafés, carry on down it as far as Enge Kerksteeg, a narrow lane to the left. It will lead you right to the entrance of the Oude Kerk.

A few views of the lively, frenetic Red-Light District.

OUDE KERK

It is the oldest and largest church in Amsterdam. The first church was built even before the
Dam: a small chapel in the form of a church rose in 1306 on the site of a wooden church erected on the east bank of the Amstel The archbishop of Utrecht consecrated it to Saint Nicholas, patron of sailors and bakers. Over the centuries, the Old Church underwent all types of alterations and restoration. In 1370 it was enlarged by building two new side chapels, but it was only in the mid-16th century that the basilica acquired its present characteristics with a nave and two aisles and the barrel vault supported by 42 pillars.

The **bell-tower** was built in 1565 according to a drawing by Joost Janszoon Bilhamer. It is 68-metres high and has a wooden spire at the top. Its 47-bell *carillon,* designed by François Hémony in 1658, is one of the most beautiful in The Netherlands. With the turbulent religious changes in 1578, the church passed into the hands of the Protestants. Calvinists removed statues, decorations and as many as 38 altars which adorned the interior of the church and which they considered a meaningless Catholic luxury. The Oude Kerk was transformed into a meeting-place for the citizens; in the 17th century the church was used more and more for non-religious purposes.

Oude Kerk – the oldest church in Amsterdam
as it is today.

Oude Kerk – the interior

The great oak organ designed
by Jan Westerman was installed
in 1724.

Three stained-glass windows
designed by Pieter Aertszoon in
1555, to be found in the
Chapel of Our Lady to the right
on entering, date back to the
Renaissance. They depict the
Death of the Virgin, the *Adora-
tion of the Shepherds* and the
Good Tidings. Many famous
Dutchmen are buried in the
Oude Kerk: Admiral Jacob van
Heemskerck, who died in
Gibraltar in a naval battle
against the English, the artist
Carel van Mander and the ex-
plorer Kilaen van Rennsselaer,
one of the founders of Nieuw
Amsterdam, the future New
York. However, the most note-
worthy tombstone here is the

one with the engraving of Saskia, indicating the burial place of Rembrandt's first wife. Another sight in the Oude Kerk area is **Trompeteersteeg**, Amsterdam's narrowest lane, together with its twin **Slapersteeg**. One can turn down it after 88 Oudezijds Voorburgwal. Set off down this canal turning left after the Oude Kerk. At no. 40 one does not see the church because it is well hidden on the last floor of a beautiful 17th century house but it is here that one finds the Amstelkring Museum.

Oude Kerk – a detail of an Aertszoon stained-glass window with the Amsterdam coat-of-arms.

The Amstelkring Museum.

Amstelkring Museum – a detail of the interior.

Opposite page: Ons'Lieve Heer op Solder, the tiny church
concealed in the attic. The altarpiece depicting
The Baptism of Christ is by Jacob de Wit.

AMSTELKRING MUSEUM

The typical, 17th century Dutch house overlooking the canal, and
which incorporates two smaller buildings to the rear, houses one
of the best-kept museums in the city and the **Ons'Lieve Heer op
Solder**, what was formerly a tiny secret church dedicated to Our
Lord in the Attic.

Between 1661 and 1663, a rich trader called Jan Hartman renovated and furnished the house on the canal according to the trends of
the moment and, like other wealthy and distinguished citizens,
opened up his home to the large community of local Roman
Catholics. In fact, Hartman had created a secret church on the upper floors of the building to allow this community the opportunity
of meeting and worshipping freely together. During the dark period of intolerance that followed the Reformation in 1578, quite a
number of secret churches were created in the city, often concealed behind anonymous-looking façades, and the Ons'Lieve
Heer op Solder is the only one of them left.

The church was enlarged in 1735 and remained in activity even after freedom of worship was restored in Holland; it was finally
closed in 1887 when construction of the St. Nicholas Church in
Prins Hendrikkade was finished.

Nowadays, Christmas mass and weddings are sometimes celebrated in the little church in the attic.

The museum, which is housed on the lower floors, was opened in
1888 and displays a series of rooms decorated and furnished in the
typical Dutch Golden Century style. Worth seeing is the *Saal*, a
drawing room that has survived practically intact to this day. Even
the kitchen and the chaplain's bedroom still have their original furniture and decorations.

36

Zeedijk – the house with the wooden façade dating back to the 16th century is one of only two left standing in the city made with inflammable materials; the other is at the Begijnhof.

Sint Nicolaaskerk – the façade.

The Oudezijds Voorburgwal, a wall with numerous coats-of-arms representing the sun, moon, a swan, ships and a lion, ends in **Zeedijk**, one of the old and ill-famed streets of the old port of Amsterdam. This corner of the town has been largely restructured: Golden Tulip built an enormous luxury hotel there right alongside the Church of Saint Nicholas. In order to visit it, leave the Zeedijk, bear left and return to the Station Square, with its nearby Church of Saint Nicholas.

SINT NICOLAASKERK

It is one of the numerous Dutch churches dedicated to the patron saint of the sailors and it has been the leading Catholic church in Amsterdam since its construction was completed in 1887. Saint Nicholas is a Neo-Renaissance basilica in the shape of a cross with a nave and two aisles. It is solemn and severe in appearance and its two Baroque crowned towers and large dome, built at the intersection between the aisles and transept, reign supreme over the whole town.

The church of Saint Nicholas is somehow connected to the miracle of Amsterdam. In fact, behind the altar and above the tabernacle is the *Crown of the Emperor Maximilian I of Austria*. It was given to the city after the sovereign went on a pilgrimage to the scene of the miracle of 1345. A man on his deathbed was taking Commu-

Sint Nicolaaskerk – another view of the church that overlooks
the Prins Hendrikkade canal.

nion, but he could not swallow the host which he then vomited.
For some incredible reason, the man did not die and the host was
thrown into the fire of a hearth. But the flames did not manage to
destroy it and since then, right throughout the Middle Ages, Amsterdam was the destination of devoted pilgrims. This procession is
depicted on the right hand side of the high altar of Saint Nicholas.

Prins Hendrikkade – a view of the canal from
the Sint Nicolaaskerk.

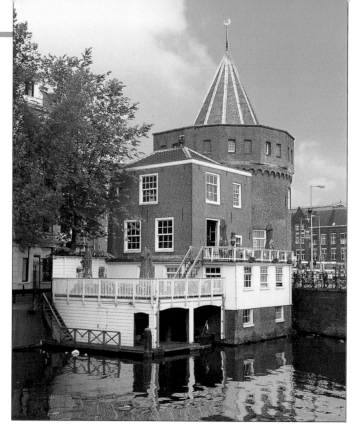

Schreierstoren – the so-called 'Tower of Tears' was originally part of the city's mediaeval walls.

From Saint Nicholas, head in the direction of Amsterdam's Ooster-dok, a dock of its huge port. And as soon as you have rounded the corner to the right of the Prins Hendrikkade, you will come face to face with the Tower of Tears.

SCHREIERSTOREN

The Tower of Tears is a fragment of the town's medieval walls which stood right in the corner where Prins Hendrikkade and **Geldersekade** intersect. This small fortress dates back to 1482: a walled plate portrays a woman and a child bidding farewell in des-peration. This was the point of departure of Amsterdam sailors for their very long voyages and here their sobbing women folk would wish them well. Another plate commemorates another important departure. Henry Hudson's *Halfmoon* set sail from Schreierstoren on the 4th April 1609; at the end of his long voyage, Hudson entered the bay that today bears his name and founded Nieuw Amsterdam, or New York. Up to 1960, the Tower of Tears housed the port administration offices whereas today it contains a wellstocked shop selling nautical goods, and a café.

From the Tower of Tears, follow the banks of one of Amsterdam's transversal canals, the enchanting Geldersekade, as far as one of the town's historical centres, **Nieuwmarkt**, which marks the boundary between Amsterdam's medieval heart and its eastern area (see page 48). Nieuwmarkt was once a very lively fish market, but today it is a large, agitated square, an imaginary boundary between the Red-Light District and the working-class areas of the centre. When the canal, which enabled the Kloveniersburgwal to join the Geldersekade, was filled in, the Public Weighhouse remained isolated and towering in the middle of Nieuwmarkt.

WAAG

It was one of the medieval gates of Amsterdam, Sint Antoniespoort, and it formed part of the town's defence system during the 15th century. An inscription recalls that the first stone of this gate was laid on the 28th April 1488.
It took Saint Anthony's Gate only two centuries to lose its original function: Amsterdam sprawled beyond it in an eastwards direction. In 1617, the internal courtyard of the gate was covered by a dome and the Public Weighhouse came into office. On the ground floor,

Waag – the St. Anthony mediaeval turreted gateway, which dominates Nieuwmarkt, was used as the Public Weighhouse for two centuries.

canons and anchors for Dutch ships were weighed. The other floors served to house some craft guilds: blacksmiths, bricklayers and artists but above all surgeons who remained there for over 200 years. They all left traces: the doctors in the **anatomical theatre**, and in the decorations of the **dome** which reproduce the coats-of-arms of their guild, the stonecutters in the decorations of their rooms and in the friezes of their entrances, sculptured by Hendrick de Keyser.

It was in this building that doctors held anatomy lessons during the 17th century. Rembrandt was invited to attend them and he took a cue from them for two of his famous paintings: *Doctor Tulp's anatomy lesson*, on exhibit at the Mauritshuis in The Hague and *Doctor Deijmann's anatomy lesson*, kept at the Rijksmuseum. The Waag has many entrances: there was so much jealousy and desire for independence on the part of the various guilds that each of them built its own separate, private entrance to its rooms.

In 1819 the old gateway ceased to house the Public Weighhouse. For many years it was used for all kinds of purposes. It risked being demolished in 1829, but then housed the Academy of Fencing before being used as a furniture storehouse. It was later transformed into a fire-station and was used in 1891 as the municipal archives. In 1926 it was the first premises of the Amsterdam Historical Museum which in 1932 gave two rooms to the Jewish Historical Museum. In 1955 this museum was enlarged to cover the whole floor and then to occupy the entire building when the Amsterdam Historical Museum moved to Kalverstraat. In 1987 the Jewish History Museum moved to even larger premises right in the middle of the Jewish District, in Jonas Daniël Meijerplein (see page 61).

This itinerary now takes us back towards the heart of Amsterdam and towards the Medieval district. From Nieuwmarkt take one of the numerous lanes on the right which lead back to the boundary

The House on Three Canals.

of the Red-Light District and towards the Oudezijds Achterburgwal, one of the inner canals of this area. Having reached this canal, bear left and go right down it. Leaving behind the last of the red lights lit up over the prostitutes' display windows, cross Oude Hoogstraat, the only busy area in this district and one of the cross-streets which lead directly to the Dam and walk slowly among the beautiful houses, until the point where the inner canals intersect. It is one of Amsterdam's most charming spots: two bridges which cut the long, transversal

Oudemanhuispoort – reading glasses are depicted over the arched entrance in Oudezijds Achterburgwal.

canals of the town's historic centre and Grimburgwal. A magnificent house featuring an antique library is emblematic of this small paradise: the **House on Three Canals** situated at their junction.

To the left of the House on Three Canals stands an arch. It is the former entrance to home for the elderly, the **Oudemanhuispoort**, today the seat of Amsterdam University. But this arcade which leads to another canal, the Kloveniersburgwal, is also famous for its book market held daily. Old gentlemen stand behind stalls worn with the passing of time, the whole gallery that permits access to the courtyard of the University is their territory. Authentic curious and very old editions are to be found.

Another view of the House on Three Canals.

Oudemanhuispoort – the arched entrance to the former home for the elderly, now the University.

UNIVERSITY

The charming inner courtyard adjacent to the booksellers' gallery was the courtyard of the old age home founded in 1601. Amsterdam University was built in 1632. On the 8th January of that same year, the historian Gerardus Johannes Vossius gave the inaugural speech of a university whose aims included opening a breach in triumphant Calvinism and defending freedom. Amsterdam University immediately attracted the most lucid minds of Dutch culture, from the mathematician Hortensius to the jurist Cabelliau and from doctor Blasius to the theologian Van Leeuwen.

In 1840 the University was transferred to this old age home and the *statue of Vossius,* first professor of Amsterdam University, was placed in the inner courtyard.

Let's walk down the Grimburgwal in the opposite direction to that of the second-hand books market. To the left is a lane with an unusual name, the **Gebed Zonder End** or Endless Prayer, which recalls the monasteries which used to exist in the neighbourhood.

The Grimburgwal forces us to leave behind the charm of the old part of Amsterdam leading us to **Rokin** one of the main streets and the continuation of Damrak. We shall come out at Rokin right where the Amstel was filled in and its course deviated. On the other side of the bridge stands a small **equestrian statue** in honour of a great queen: Wilhelmina, one of the sovereigns best loved by the Dutch. She came to the throne when she was still a girl and reigned for over fifty years, including the exile of London when the Nazis invaded Holland. In 1948 she abdicated in favour of her daughter Juliana. It was she who bestowed the motto "Heroic, resolute, courageous city" on Amsterdam's coat-of-arms. Wilhelmina's statue turns its back on the archaeological museum, the Allard Pierson Museum.

The University – the inner courtyard.

The statue of Queen Wilhelmina on horseback, in Rokin.

ALLARD PIERSON MUSEUM

When it was clear that the city of Amsterdam had the possibility of coming into possession of the important private collection of the archaeologist Scheurleer, it was decided that the time had come to create an archaeological museum. This took place in 1934 and the museum was dedicated to the humanist Allard Pierson. Since 1976 it has been located in the old building of the Dutch National Bank, 127 Oude Turfmarkt.

Unlike many archeological museums, the Allard Pierson is not large, but its collections are very valuable and cover entire periods of history of Western and Middle Eastern civilizations. On the ground floor are treasures of *Ancient Egypt*: mummies, funeral masks and sculptures in stone and bronze alongside precious *collections from Middle Eastern Asia*. The top floor displays *Greek art*, but also *bronzes* and *Etruscan funeral urns*. It is also worth mentioning the *Roman collection* grouped around a gigantic sarcophagus in marble dating back to the 2nd century A.D.

The entrance to the Allard Pierson Museum.

Allard Pierson Museum – its Neo-classic façade.

Allard Pierson Museum

45

Zuiderkerkhof
•p. 48

Montelbaanstoren
•p. 52

Nieuwmarkt • Oostindisch Huis • Trippenhuis •
Zuiderkerk • Pintohuis • Montelbaanstoren •
West Jerusalem • Museum Het Rembrandthuis •
Waterlooplein • Flea Market • Mozes en Aäronkerk •
Portuguese Synagogue • Statue of the dockworker •
Joods Historisch Museum

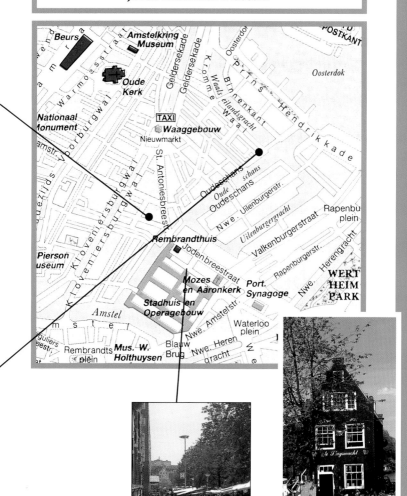

Flea Market
•p. 58

Sint Antoniesluis
•p. 52

NIEUWMARKT

Today Nieuwmarkt is a sort of Dutch Beaubourg which is for more than a single building as in the case of Paris, but involves an entire district. On walking down Hoogstraat, the old houses of Amsterdam suddenly disappear, giving way to futurist outlines and unusual colours: blue, yellow, green and white. Houses and buildings in glass, varnished iron and unfinished concrete; the new erupts into town-planning in Nieuwmarkt and boldly fits in with the most classic buildings in Amsterdam. Nieuwmarkt is recent history in Amsterdam. During the seventies, the local government decided to build an underground. An undertaking with prohibitive financial and social costs: any underground building operation in a city built on piles is impossible without completely demolishing the preexisting constructions. This was the destiny of all the houses under which the underground was to pass and also the destiny of Nieuwmarkt, one of the most populated districts in Amsterdam, once inhabited by workers and dockworkers but since 1975 mainly by young people.

The inhabitants of Nieuwmarkt rebelled against the decision to destroy it: nobody wanted to leave and nobody wanted his house destroyed; for months, police and bulldozers clashed with thousands of youngsters who fought tooth and nail against the underground project.

Despite strong opposition, houses were demolished and one of the districts was even razed to the ground. However, once the destruction had been terminated, construction works of new houses started immediately. This gave a completely new look to Nieuwmarkt: houses in glass and cement with strange, modular structures, whose amortization costs are paid by the State which supplements the difference as against the rents paid by inhabitants, who have largely returned to live in their old district.

Nowadays, wandering around the streets of Nieuwmarkt (Sint Antoniebreestraat, Hoogstraat, Zuiderkerkhof and Raamgracht) is like entering a new city. In Nieuwmark one comes across some charming sights; for instance, Zuiderkerkhof, where the old clashes with the new because the exterior of the old apse of the Zuiderkerk is surrounded by modern, elegant buildings.

The subway station in Nieuwmarkt Square, next to the Public Weighhouse, is a veritable monument and the only one of its kind. By means of panels and sculptures, it narrates the history of Nieuwmarkt from the time of Rembrandt right up to modern times. An enormous steel ball can been seen above the panels: this is the work of Jan Sierhuis, one of the leading contemporary Dutch artists.

OOSTINDISCH HUIS

The University now owns this building in Oude Hoogstraat 24, on the corner of Kloveniersburgwal, but it was once the headquarters of the powerful Dutch East Indes Company. However, there is no plaque on the building to indicate this; the only thing left that connects it with the trading that took place between this company and the Far East, and which contributed so greatly to the wealth of the country, is a small VOC crest in an inner courtyard beyond the front door.

Attributed to Hendrick de Keyser, the building still boasts practically all of its original façade, whereas the interiors were substantially modified during various moments of renovation at the end of the 19th century, when the structure was used for other purposes. The VOC kept it as its headquarters until the company was dissolved in 1800.

At no. 12 Kloveniersburgwal, take a look at Jacob Hooy's **chemist-herbalist shop**. One of Amsterdam's historic shops dating back to 1743, over 400 herbs are on sale here in a pleasant atmosphere, both, for medical and cooking purposes. At **no. 29**, on the other side of the canal, stands the Trippenhuis, one of the most impressive and famous houses of Amsterdam.

Above: Oostindisch Huis, the building that was the headquarters of the VOC for almost two centuries. It now belongs to Amsterdam University.

Below: the antique Jacob Hooy & Co. chemist-herbalist shop.

Trippenhuis – the stately Neo-classic town house is actually two buildings in one. A row of fake windows flanked by Corinthian columns can be seen on the façade.

Below: the tiny Trippenhuis, one the narrowest houses in Amsterdam. The cornice with two sphinxes is very picturesque.

TRIPPENHUIS

The house of the Trips is a real neoclassic palace. It was built by one of the greatest 17th century architects, Justus Vingboons, for the Trip brothers, Lodewijk and Hendrick, stone-rich cannon manufactures and owners of iron mines in Sweden. They were the grandsons of Louis de Geer, Holland's iron king in the 17th centu-

ry. They wanted a house in keeping with their enormous wealth and managed to have one built between 1660 and 1664. They were not ungrateful to the family business that enabled such luxury: the *chimneys* of the Trippenhuis are in the shape of huge mortars.

Even after the end of the Trip family's industrial empire, their house remained one of the most important in Amsterdam; following the abdication of Louis Bonaparte, William the First decided in 1816 to transfer the Royal Palace collections to the Trippenhuis, where they remained until Queen Wilhelmina.

A small house, an exact miniature copy of the Trippenhuis, stands on the opposite bank of the canal at no. 26; the **tiny Trippenhuis** was the home of one the Trip servants who, after having let slip one day that all he needed to be happy was a house the size of the main door of the Trippenhuis, received the miniature copy as a present from one of the Trip brothers.

Zuiderkerk – the bell-tower.

The archway that links Sint Antoniebreestraat with the small Zuiderkerk Square.

The façade of the Pintohuis; the building houses the Openbare Bibliotheek.

ZUIDERKERK

Built in 1603 by the ever-present Hendrick de Keyser, the Zuiderkerk or South Church is a Protestant church dominated by a high bell-tower; during the summer months, it is possible to climb up it. The Zuiderkerk is reliving today a new golden era after decades of abandon; in 1929, in fact, the last religious services were held there. The parish was becoming depopulated and the ecclesiastic authorities decided to suppress services in the Zuiderkerk. Nowadays, after many years of restoration, the Zuiderkerk is used for cultural events.
Access is gained to the Zuiderkerk through a small arch crowned by a skull. It is to be found between nos. 130 and 132 of Sint Antoniebreestraat.

At no. 69 of the same street is a library, the **Openbare Bibliotheek**. As a matter of fact, it is another of Amsterdam's famous houses: the **Pintohuis**. De Pinto was a rich Jewish banker who arrived in Amsterdam at the beginning of the 17th century. It was the city's golden era and De Pinto wasted no time in making a fortune. He bought this lovely house in 1651 and remodelled its façade and interior according to classic criteria. Isaac De Pinto's wealth was proverbial: when the inhabitants of the entire Jewish quarter wanted to emphasize someone's wealth, they would say "rich as De Pinto". During the seventies while the houses

SINT ANTONIESLUIS
26 t/m 37

around De Pinto's residence were being demolished, his old, luxurious house, was restored, bringing the sumptuous decorations of the interior back to their former glory.

Continuing along Sint Antoniebreestraat, you will reach one of Amsterdam's most photographed corners: the **Sint Antoniesluis**, the weir on the **Oudeschans** one of the widest canals in which the Amstel was deviated. The view from this weir is worth stopping for. The final stretch of the Oudeschans is dominated by a squat tower: the Montelbaanstoren.

MONTELBAANSTOREN

It is a red-brick tower. It was built in 1512 purely for defence reasons. It had to protect the Lastage, the basin for repairing and storing big Dutch ships. It was merely a lowered tower; in 1606, Hendrick de Keyser added its spire. Today this tower houses the offices in charge of the closing of canals and water flow in Amsterdam.

A view of the Zuiderkerk from Jodenbreestraat.

The Montelbaanstoren, the tower erected on the banks of the Oudeschans in 1512.
Hendrick de Keyser added the elegant bell-tower in the 17th century.

Sint Antoniesluis, the weir on the Oudeschans.

WEST JERUSALEM

For centuries, this was Amsterdam's nickname. From the 16th century onwards the Dutch capital was the only possible refuge for thousands of Jews persecuted right throughout Europe. For them Amsterdam represented the "Mokum", the only safe city in which to live. The first Jews to take refuge there escaped the Catholic Inquisition. They came from Spain and wanted to call themselves Sephardis, from the Jewish name for the Iberian peninsula. Subsequently, after the fall of Antwerp (1585), the Jewish traders from those towns, who managed to survive, arrived; they were the first diamond cutters to live in Amsterdam. From then onwards, Jewish migration to Amsterdam never ceased. Poor, destitute Jews, the Ashkenazi, arrived in thousands from Germany and Eastern European countries. The two worlds clashed: the Sephardis formed a well-off merchant middle-class, while the German communities struggled in hopeless poverty. The doors of many occupations were closed to them.

The end of the 17th century represented a period of exceptional population growth for Amsterdam; in the space of a century the city accepted refugees from all over Europe increasing its population fourfold.

The first Jews to reach the Dutch capital settled in the eastern part of Amsterdam, behind the narrow towers of Sint Antoniespoort, which was later to house the Public Scales. They went to live around the large square of Waterlooplein. In no time at all the Jews formed a powerful merchant class. If in 1672 there were scarcely 10,000 in a town of almost 200,000 inhabitants, at the beginning of the 20th century, there were over 60,000 Jews in Amsterdam. In the thirties, they were joined by communities fleeing from Nazi Germany. They were not safe for long; in 1940, Hitler invaded Holland and only waited a year before starting his racial persecution.

Sint Antoniesluis is the point of access to **Jodenbreestraat**, the real heart of the Jewish district. At the beginning of the 20th century, 95% of its inhabitants were Jewish. Jodenbreestraat was the district's business thoroughfare. A large section of its northern part was demolished in 1955, making it lose its charm. But the first house of this wide street is still famous throughout the world.

MUSEUM HET REMBRANDTHUIS

Nos. 4-6 Jodenbreestraat are occupied by what was Rembrandt's house for almost twenty years, which has since been turned into a museum dedicated to him. When Rembrandt, the greatest Dutch painter, decided to live in Amsterdam, he rented a house at the corner of what was to become Jodenbreestraat. It belonged to Hendrick van Uylenburg, who traded in paintings. It was in this house that Rembrandt, when he was still unknown, met his first wife, Saskia an orphan, and relation of the owners of his house and daughter of the old burgomaster of Leeuwarden. It was a good marriage for Rembrandt; Saskia's ancestors belonged to some of the greatest families of Friesland and she opened the doors of the upper merchant classes of Amsterdam.

Rembrandt and Saskia lived in several houses which they rented before returning to live in the painter's former house. In fact, in 1639, Rembrandt decided to buy the house alongside his first residence in the town's new district which was spreading eastwards. Rembrandt's new house had been built in 1606: a typical middle-class double storey. The artist paid 13,000 guilders for it. It was not

Rembrandt's house and museum – the inner courtyard of the building.

Opposite page: the façade of Rembrandt's house and museum.

a fantastic amount yet Rembrandt never managed to pay it off entirely. The period in which he lived in this house was magic. He was already a famous artist with important commissions. He lived on the ground floor, using the first floor as a studio. His pupils and aids worked in the attic.

Rembrandt was a keen collector and filled his house with all sorts of valuable objects: he managed to collect more than one hundred paintings on the ground floor alone and in the other rooms he collected drawings, pottery, Japanese weapons, shells, coral and even exotic clothing.

These were happy, busy years which sadly enough were destined to end: three of his children died leaving only his fourth child, Titus, and in 1642 his fragile wife, Saskia, died at the age of thirty-two, while the artist's economic situation was shaky.

In 1645, Rembrandt remarried and his energetic new wife, Hendrickje Stoffels, tried to solve his financial problems. But by this stage, the situation was out of hand and Rembrandt could no longer pay off his debts.

In the space of two years, between 1657 and 1658, he was obliged to sell all his collections (getting nothing for them) as well as his house. The Rembrandts moved to the poor district of the Jordaan and his wife, together with his son Titus, opened a shop selling objets d'art. In this way, Rembrandt abandoned the Jewish quarter in which his masterpieces matured and where the famous *Night watch* was painted.

The house in which he lived also underwent profound transformations: in 1660 it was raised by a storey and its façade was redesigned according to classicist models.

Rembrandt's house and museum – the artist's studio.

In 1906, for the third centenary celebrations of Rembrandt's birth, the city of Amsterdam purchased this house for the purpose of making it into a museum; it was opened to the public in 1911.

Interior – The atmosphere of the museum is sensational: all the windows are screened and the light is softened to avoid damaging the magnificent collection of etchings on display. The museum underwent accurate renovation in 1999, when the interiors were restored as faithfully as possible to what they must have looked like when Rembrandt lived there. In fact, the rooms are furnished and decorated with original pieces from the 17thcentury.
The only permanent exhibition in the world of the entire collection of Rembrandt's etchings is to be found in the new wing. The museum also holds work by some of the artist's contemporaries, by his pupils and by his teacher, Pieter Lastman.

The Stadhuis-Muziektheater in the Waterlooplein area.
This building has always been the object of fierce criticism by the citizens, to the extent that it has been nicknamed the 'Stopera', which is a contraction of the word 'Stadhuis' (Town Hall) and Opera House – but the underlying meaning is... Stop the Opera!

Leaving Rembrandthuis behind and continuing down Joden-breestraat, on the left-hand side of the street we come across an underground passage: this leads into **Uilenburg**, which was one of the most poverty-stricken areas of the city during the 16th century. The most destitute of the refugees arriving in the city found shelter here; large families with ten or even more children packed them-selves into the dingy, decaying houses. Substantial slum clearance was started on the district in 1926.
Near a synagogue in Nieuwe Uilenburgerstraat we come across the large Gassan diamond laboratories, which re-opened in 1989 after years of inactivity and considerable transformation.
Back on Jodenbreestraat again, we now head for the Water-looplein area.

WATERLOOPLEIN

A significant amount of construction performed over recent years has changed the appearance of this square, once the centre of the Jewish district and since 1986 dominated by the imposing building that houses the **Stadhuis-Muziektheater**, that is, the Town Hall and the Opera Theatre. It is one of the most controversial construc-tions in Amsterdam and denigrators have re-named it the 'Stopera'

FLEA MARKET

In Amsterdam's most famous market, you can find literally everything amongst confusion and continuous bartering. They will try to sell you an old gramophone with no hope of working, broken records, worn-out books, second-hand clothes and trinkets. But, with a bit of patience and luck, you might manage to find something you have been searching for in vain for years. But do not expect to find great bargains: the vendors are fully aware of the value of their goods. And it is quite understandable; they have a century-old experience behind them. The first Jewish merchants to inaugurate the flea market did so over one hundred years ago: in 1883 when Waterlooplein was protected against recurrent floods which occurred each time the Amstel was full. Right throughout the morning, Amsterdam's flea market is full of people who protest, contract, buy and ruin themselves in order to buy chips of a glorious past or search for missing cooking utensils which cost too much in the shops. The flea market is one of the places in which to idle away one's time.

Having reached Waterlooplein, turn left; on the corner of the square, bordering on Mr. Visserplein, stands the Neo-classic Moses and Aäron Church.

Waterlooplein – the monument commemorating the Jews who lost their lives during the Second World War.

The Waterlooplein Flea Market, which started in 1883.

The Moses and Aäron Church – the figures of these two biblical characters were originally on the church façade and are now on the rear.

The Moses and Aäron Church – the Neo-classic façade.

MOZES EN AÄRONKERK

The history of this church is somewhat unique. It dates back to the period in which the Catholic religion was persecuted after the Protestant Reform. A rich, devoted Catholic, Boelenz bought the House of Moses and Aäron at the corner of **Jodenbreestraat** from a Jewish mercant and converted it into a secret chapel where he reunited companions of the same faith. Over the centuries, the church was enlarged until it reached its present dimensions. It was consecrated only in 1841 after a Belgian architect had built its compact neoclassic **façade** with four massive columns crowned by a *statue of Christ*. Two twin towers rise up at the sides of the roof balustrade. The interior is baroque and gloomy, but the Church of Moses and Aäron ceased to hold religious services some time ago. It is a sort of social centre where yoga courses, concerts, festivals and showmarts are held. It is also a meeting place for foreigners working in Amsterdam who find assistance here for their problems. In October, the wide spaces of the church are filled with all types of animals for the World Animal's Day.

The Portuguese Synagogue.

We come out of Moses and Aäron into **Mr. Visserplein**, a vast square, at the sides of which stand the most important synagogues in Amsterdam. On the right hand side of the square stands the Huiszittenhuis, the almshouse owned by the town government. In 1632 Spinoza, son of a Jewish Portuguese trader, and one of the most fertile Western thinkers was born at **no. 61** of this square.

PORTUGUESE SYNAGOGUE

One of the most beautiful synagogues in the world, it was built between 1671 and 1675 by Elias Bouman and looks like a gigantic cube in dark red brick, surrounded by a row of low houses built very close to one another. The south east façade of the synagogue faces Jerusalem and its whole structure was modelled on the example of the Temple of Solomon.

The **interior** in baroque style is formed by a single, large hall covered by three wooden barrel vaults supported by four columns. Enormous chandeliers, which are lit for Jewish religious holidays, hang from these vaults. The **women's gallery** is supported by twelve columns that symbolize the tribes of Israel. The *Chest* containing Torah's scrolls is worth taking a look at. The low houses encircling the Portuguese synagogue contain one of the most famous libraries in the world: **Ets Haim**, "The Tree of Life", where valuable volumes covering the whole history of Spanish and Portuguese Jews in all its complexity can be consulted.

The statue of the dockworker, in Jonas Daniël Meijerplein.

Below: the Jewish History Museum and the Star of David outside one of the entrances.

The statue of the dock worker – It is attributed to Mari Andriessen, but its significance goes beyond its artistic value. It is the statue that Amsterdam dedicated to the dockworkers' strike proclaimed in February 1941 against the first deportations of Jews in Germany. The whole city came to a halt following the example of the dockers and even today on the 25th February of every year the inhabitants of Amsterdam gather around this statue in memory of that day.

JOODS HISTORISCH MUSEUM

The Jewish History Museum complex, opened in Jonas Daniël Meijerplein in 1987, is actually four 17th and 18th Ashkenazy synagogues, beautifuly restored between 1980 and 1990 and linked to each other by means of a series of covered pathways. These four buildings are the Great Synagogue (1671), the High Synagogue (1685), the Third Synagogue (1700) and the New Synagogue (1752).

The museum is articulated in themes according to the various aspects of Jewish history and culture.

The **Great Synagogue** holds the white marble *Sacred Ark* donated by Rabbi Abraham Auerbach when the temple was opened.

The various showcases display objects used for worship as well as items in silver, clothing, and a 17th century Torah mantle. The *mikveh,* the tub used for ritual bathing, is preserved in one of the side rooms.

The **New Synagogue** contains the wooden *Sacred Ark* brought here from Enkhuizen. Another interesting item is the *Hoggadah Manuscript*, which contains a beautiful collection of illuminations done by Joseph from Leipnik in 1734.

Singelgracht
•p. 71

Begijnhof
•p. 68

Bloemenmarkt
•p. 71

Magere Brug
•p. 76

Kalverstraat • Amsterdams Historisch Museum •
Begijnhof • Bloemenmarkt • Muntplein • Munttoren •
Tuschinski Theater • Rembrandtplein • Blauwbrug •
Magere Brug • Willet-Holthuysen Museum•
Antique Dealers'District

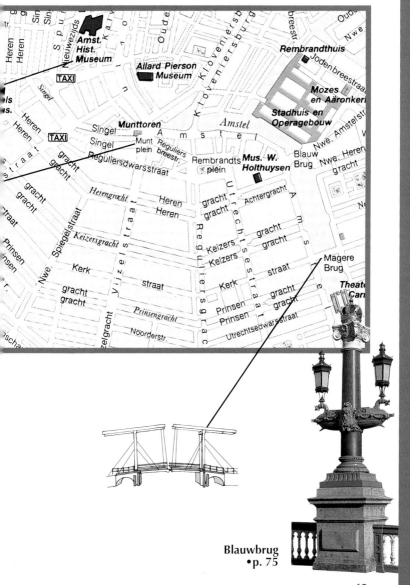

Blauwbrug
•p. 75

KALVERSTRAAT

Kalverstraat, Amsterdam's most crowded street, starts from the Damsquare. On Saturdays, real human walls move along this commercial street blocked to traffic which joins the Dam to Muntplein. It is a very old street: it already existed in 1393 when breeders passed along it to take their animals to the Dam market. This gave rise at the time to the first shops and workshops. They were opened by butchers, whose example was soon followed by carpenters, shoemakers and basket-weavers. In 1800 over 200 shops had been opened in the Kalverstraat, which has become in recent years the favourite destination for a hundred thousand people who invade it daily to do hurried shopping. With the passing of time, Kalverstraat has lost a great deal of its fascination, becoming an agitated street full of large department stores, fastfoods and boutiques: a commer-

cial street like many others in Europe. With a great exception: the "Maison de Bonneterie" at no. 183. In 1889 two Jewish traders, Josef Cohen and Rose Wittegenstein, opened their knitwear shop on this spot. They were lucky: in 1911 they enlarged their premises occupying a whole, lovely building. The war swept them away and all Jewish textile traders were obliged by the Nazis to deposit all their wares in the old Maison de Bonneterie. Two plates at the entrance to each floor of the Maison commemorate the founders of the company and the staff who were killed during the Second World War. Today the Maison de Bonneterie is an elegant department store finely decorated in late 19th century style. In the vast galleries and in the large hall are to be found quality articles of clothing and signed outfits. Furthermore, a small café faces the Rokin.

AMSTERDAMS HISTORISCH MUSEUM

At number 92 Kalverstraat a stone arch leads to the courtyards of the old orphanage or Burgerweeshuis of Amsterdam, today occupied by the Amsterdam Historical Museum. The building was built as a monastery dedicated to Saint Lucy and remained as such for over one hundred years, from 1414 to 1578.
It was only then that the building underwent its first radical transformation, lodging the city's orphans. This situation lasted for over four centuries: in 1960 the orphanage closed its doors to open them fifteen years

later, on the seven hundredth anniversary of Amsterdam, as the prestigious premises of the City Historical Museum.

Through the arch on Kalverstraat (on which are engraved verses by the poet Van den Vondel) one gains access to the **boys' courtyard**. To the left you will see cupboards where the orphans put their overalls and tools back after a day's work, while to the right, the old granary of the convent now houses a restaurant, "In de Oude Goliath."

Its interior is dominated by the gigantic *statue of Goliath* flanked by the tiny *David*. From 1650 to 1682, Goliath was the main attraction of Amsterdam's amusement park: thanks to a simple device, his eyes roll and his head moves.

From the **girls' courtyard** which follows on the boys' courtyard, one gains access to the museum.

Amsterdam Historical Museum – plaques on the wall at the Kalverstraat entrance.

Amsterdam Historical Museum – the entrance from St. Luciensteeg.

Opposite page: Amsterdam Historical Museum – the arched entrance from Kalverstraat.

Amsterdams Historisch Museum

Interior – The Amsterdam Historical Museum narrates the tales of the city from prehistoric times to the present day. The rapid growth of Amsterdam, its port, the fortunes of the Golden Century and minor events of daily life are narrated across the numerous halls describing the continuous struggle of the inhabitants of Amsterdam against the sea.

Having undergone extensive renovation in 1999, the newly furbished wing equipped with up-to-date interactive technologies offers an extraordinary presentation of the city's history from 1815 to this day.

Do not fail to take a look outside the other entrance to the building: in St. Luciensteeg, in a wall to the left of the door, 22 coats-of-arms of Amsterdam are walled.

In front of the girls' courtyard, a gallery which is unique in the world, the **Civil Guards' Gallery**, enables one to move towards the entrance to the Begijnhof. In no other city on earth are very valuable, historic paintings on display in a passage open to the public. The Civil Guards' Gallery contains paintings depicting militia formed in the 14th century to defend traders.

Opposite page: Amsterdam Historical Museum – views of the boys' courtyard.

Amsterdam Historical Museum – two views of the girls' courtyard and, bottom right, the entrance to the Civil Guards' Gallery.

BEGIJNHOF

Begijnhof – the entrance from Gedempte Begijnensloot.

It is a place of absolute quiet, an idyllic oasis and an unexpected refuge from the uproar of Kalverstraat.

Coming out of the Municipal Police Gallery, one comes across a gate to the right. In Gedempte Begijnensloot is one of the entrances to the Begijnhof leading to a sort of vast **courtyard** in the centre of which is a lovely lawn surrounded by numerous small houses kept in perfect order. Old ladies who go for strolls and drink tea in their gardens, flowers everywhere, an incredible sense of calm and two chapels facing one another together form the Begijnhof.

It was founded in 1346 by a group of women, beguines, who aspired to living in a religious community without restricting themselves to the rigid rules of a cloistered life. They did not take the vow and behaved as lay sisters: they all kept their own little houses, personal liberty and freedom but they dedicated their lives to the poor and ill.

Begijnhof – houses facing on to the well-kept gardens and courtyard.

In 1578 the Protestant Reform deprived the beguines of their chapel which was then assigned to the Presbyterians. It is the church still standing in the centre of the Begijnhof. Protestantism did not bend the community who remained Catholic and the beguines continued to hold their religious services, changing house each time in order not to be discovered. The **Catholic chapel** in front of the **English church** is just an old house transformed into a place of worship.

Begijnhof – the bronze statue of a beguine, on front of the wooden house.

Begijnhof – the oldest wooden house in the city (around 1420).

At number 34 of the Begijnhof is situated the **oldest house in Amsterdam**, one of the two still in wood after an order of the city government prevented the construction of new houses in inflammable materials. The house at number 34 dates back to the 15th century and the blind wall to the left shows some beautiful tablets with scenes from the Bible.

Begijnhof – the biblical theme plaques on the wall, next to the house at no. 34, and the doorway on Spui.

Begijnhof

69

Every year on the 2nd May, visitors to the Begijnhof can observe flowers placed on a dark stone, to the side of the English church. It is the simple *tomb of Cornelia Arents.* On her death, this beguine asked for a simple burial to expiate the guilt of her family who had been converted to Protestantism. Her wish was not granted and Cornelia was initially placed inside the church, but in the morning the coffin containing Cornelia's body was found outside the chapel door. This phenomenon recurred three times until this beguine's dying wishes were fulfilled. Today beguines no longer live here. The last of them died in 1971 and the Begijnhof lodges poor old ladies on their own who pay a nominal rent. Alongside the old wooden house at number 34 is the exit to the Begijnhof which opens onto the **Spui**.

The building in front is the **Maagdenhuis**, the House of the Virgins. It used to be a Catholic orphanage built in 1787. Today it belongs to Amsterdam University. On turning to the right, proceed in the direction of one of the intellectual centres of the Dutch capital. In the centre stands a tiny, mocking statue, **Het Lieverdje**, the Amsterdam's impertinent "urchin", one of the city's ironic symbols. Behind the statue of the rogue is one of Amsterdam's best bookshops, the Athenaeum, alongside one of the most popular cafés, the "Hoppe," a very crowded meeting place for both students and artists, often written up by writers and journalists.

The street to the right of the Hoppe, Heisteeg, leads to the **Singel** the innermost canal in Amsterdam.

'The little urchin', a statue by Carel Kneulman, in Spui Square.

The picturesque Hoppe café, a frequent meeting place for artists and intellectuals.

BLOEMENMARKT

The picturesque flower market is held daily on some fifteen or so barges moored along the Singel, just a short distance from Munttoren.

It quite probably dates back to the latter half of the 19th century, when blooms and plants were sold directly from the boats tied up at the canal banks and by the growers themselves, who afterwards went back to their fields.

This is now the only flower market in Amsterdam and is always very busy, not only with tourists on the look out for the famous Dutch tulip bulbs but also with the local citizens, who are extremely fond of botany. It is a lively and cheerful floral bazaar, where you can find almost everything from exotic banana trees to yucca plants, from coconut palms to papyrus and, of course, bonsai shrubs and trees.

71

MUNTPLEIN

At the end of the Flower Market is another of Amsterdam's hubs: Muntplein, one of the city's compulsory intersections. Seven streets meet at Muntplein, a square from which some of the most famous streets such as Kalverstraat, Rokin or Reguliersbreestraat lead. In Muntplein, which more than a real square is a large bridge between the Singel and the Amstel, stands the **Munttoren**, the Mint Tower. It is a large baroque tower built in 1620 by the architect, Hendrick de Keyser right where the Regulierspoort, one of the oldest gates in Amsterdam, used to stand. When Louis XIV's armies invaded Holland in 1672, the Dutch government decided to transfer from French-occupied Utrecht to Amsterdam the state mint which was lodged in this very tower which formed part of the city's vast defence system.

The Munttoren was damaged during one of Amsterdam's frequent fires. All that remained was a squat stump in which they built a spire, which still rises up above the jerky traffic of Muntplein.

Muntplein – the imposing Munttoren, or National Mint Tower.

Today the Mint Tower houses one of the most prestigious Delft ceramic shops, "De Porceleyne Fles," the only one in Amsterdam offering every single piece of the vast original production of the Delft factory.

Another of the city's very busy streets that branches off from the Muntplein intersection is **Reguliersbreestraat.** This modern thoroughfare full of shops and offices is the area where Dutch homosexuals meet in their favourite haunts, but it is also the street for pizza restaurants, snack bars and video-game amusement halls, and runs parallel to the exclusive **Reguliersdwarsstraat** which is an entirely different environment. When in Reguliersbreestraat, do not fail to have a look at what may be considered a rather unusual stopping place for a tourist: the **Tuschinski Theater.** Do not hesitate, go into the large hall and sit down for a cup of coffee while you enjoy the warm atmosphere of exotic carpets and impeccable details and decorations. Ever since it was opened in 1921, the Tuschinski has always attracted and fascinated visitors because of its pleasant blend of art déco and elements designed by the Amsterdam School of Architecture. It was the masterpiece of one of the great pioneers in theatrics, a Polish Jew called Abraham Tuschinski, who personally and almost maniacally followed every detail concerning this palace cinema. His *bust* stands out against a star spangled blue background behind the bar counter, beside those of the first owners of the theatre, Ehrlich and Gerschtanowitz. Unfortunately, Tuschinski did not escape the Nazis: he died at Auschwitz in 1942, but his cinema-theatre is still one of the most astonishing in Europe.

Reguliersbreestraat leads into Rembrandtplein.

Munttoren – one of the statues.

Tuschinski Theater – details of the art déco façade.

REMBRANDTPLEIN

It is a crowded square during the day and noisy at night. Together with Leidseplein, it is one of Amsterdam's pulsating centres. Whereas Leidseplein is a great attraction for young people, open air-plays and new musical trends, Rembrandtplein is full of café-chantants, restaurants, night-clubs, discotheques and striptease joints. Rembrandtplein was the setting for a famous market selling poultry and dairy products. It was known as the Butter market, or *Botermarkt*. It became a meeting place and a square of happy confusion. It was capable of maintaining this atmosphere even when the market was no longer held there. It changed its name when the **statue of Rembrandt**, sculptured by Royer in 1852, was erected there in 1876.

Famous cafés and bars are dotted around Rembrandtplein and the adjoining **Thorbeckeplein**: the Old Bell, the famous Schiller, which before the war was a favourite haunt for Jewish intellectuals, the Rhapsody and brightly lit, imposing Pink Elephant alongside good restaurants for all tastes and pockets. Rembrandtplein also seems to have no limits to what it can offer. Even the smallest **police station** in the world on the corner with Reguliersbreestraat, a little lane called Halvemaansteeg, with some of the most popular gay cafés in town and the *statue of Thorbecke*, a statesman of the 19th century, ill at ease amidst the excitement that animates Rembrandtplein.

Rembrandt's statue and the many open-air cafés in Rembrandtplein.

At this point we are only a short distance away from the River Amstel, one of the most fascinating parts of Amsterdam and around which the origins of the city were founded.

BLAUWBRUG

The Blauwbrug, or Blue Bridge, owes its name to a bridge that no longer exists and which was painted in the characteristic blue of the Dutch flag. However, it kept its name also after 1883 when it was replaced by the spans of a new bridge which is none other than an exact copy of the Alexandre III bridge in Paris. It was a strange, architectural decision that did not fail to spark off disputes among the inhabitants of Amsterdam who were not used to the excessive refinement of this new bridge that contrasted with all the others, which were more functional than beautiful.

The Blauwburg on the Amstel with its sculpted decorations and lamps that make it reminiscent of the Alexander III bridge in Paris.

Brug open motor af !

MAGERE BRUG

The Blauwbrug also has an awkward neighbour to measure up with: the **Magere Brug**. You can see it spanning the Amstel, to your right. This bridge, the most photographed in Amsterdam, is the last of the hundreds of wooden bridges that once crossed the city's canals. It is a drawbridge measuring over 80 metres from bank to bank, and is forever in function to allow the canal barges to pass through underneath it. When it was first built it was just a narrow footbridge, and this is probably why it was known as the 'thin' bridge, 'mager' being the Dutch word for thin. Another tale woven around this curious name narrates that it was built to satisfy the wishes of the two Mager sisters who, living on opposite banks of the Amstel, could then avoid a long walk when visiting each other. Whichever is the true origin of its name, it definitely is the most famous and picturesque bridge in Amsterdam, especially at night, when it is all lit up. In 1722 it was widened into a double drawbridge. The Magere Brug we see today was built in 1969 and its mechanisms are still worked by hand.

The picturesque Magere Brug, the most famous drawbridge in the city.

WILLET-HOLTHUYSEN MUSEUM

Go in the back entrance, leading from the small, ornamental gardens facing Amstelstraat. The main entrance is on the other side at no. 605 Herengracht. The Herengracht was the "gentlemen's canal", and the Willet-Holthuysen is typical of these stupendous homes.

This house was built in 1687 by Jacob Hop, a diplomat and town counsellor. For two centuries it was inhabited by upper middle-class families, including one of Amsterdam's burgomasters, Willem Gideon Deutz van Assendelft, who made various changes to the house. In 1858, after passing through numerous hands, this house on the Herengracht was inherited by Louise Holthuysen, who then married Abraham Willet, a great art lover. It was a hobby his wife shared and encouraged. Willet, who was already a great book-lover, became a tireless collector of ceramics, paintings, silverware and artistic glass.

The entrance to the Willet-Holthuysen Museum.

The couple had no children and did not wish to scatter the collections of a lifetime; therefore they gave their personal property to the city of Amsterdam together with the sum of 200 thousand guilders, on condition that their house was transformed into a museum bearing their name. On the 1st May 1896 this extraordinary little museum opened its doors, but did not achieve great success. It was neglected by the city administration. In fact, rumour has it that this was the only quiet place where young sweethearts could meet without being disturbed. It is only recently that the real value of this house was appreciated: the Willet-Holthuysen museum is a perfect example of a rich house in Amsterdam, evidence of century-old wealth, and of upper middle-class style that reflects good taste and refinement.

Interior – The atmosphere of this house on the Herengracht is unforgettable. Its **dining room** in the magnificent 17th century furnishing originally belonging to the Willets, its ground floor **kitchen** with its antique utensils, its **blue room** with its walls covered in Utrecht velvet worked on original rollers and its **garden**, an example of delicate landscape gardening of the early 18th century, contribute to making a visit to the Willet's house a step back into the splendours of an Amsterdam created by intelligent lovers of beauty.

The splendid French garden is now double in size than the original one, and was laid out in 1972.

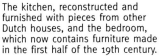

The kitchen, reconstructed and furnished with pieces from other Dutch houses, and the bedroom, which now contains furniture made in the first half of the 19th century.

The well-appointed blue room, and the corridor displaying sixteen painted decorations by Paul Colin, some of which are copies of work by famous 18th century French artists.

Amstelkerk – the tiny wooden church, erected in the 17th century and designed by Daniël Stalpaert, which faces on to the Prinsengracht.

Nieuwe Spiegelstraat.

Quaint antique shops in the Nieuwe
Spiegelstraat district.

NIEUWE SPIEGEL
STRAAT CENTRUM

ANTIQUE DEALERS' DISTRICT

Continuing along the Herengracht, aften Vijzelstraat, you will reach
Nieuwe Spiegelstraat, another of Amsterdam historic streets. Probably there is no other place in the world with such an extraordinary
concentration of antique shops. It is a street no longer than 300
metres, but where almost one hundred antique dealers have managed to find space, displaying precious collections, from the rarest
such as music boxes to the best-known such as furniture.
Nieuwe Spiegelstraat is the street that leads directly to the **Rijksmuseum** and the history of this district of antique dealers is closely
connected to that of the most famous Dutch museum. Only two
years had passed since Queen Wilhelmina inaugurated the
Rijksmuseum collections (1885) when the first antique dealer
opened his doors on that route, lost between fields and canals,
which led to the new museum. This was the spark: shops sprung up
like mushrooms along the Spiegelstraat until the commercial ex-
plosions of 1960 and 1970.

Stedelijk Museum
•p. 98

Van Gogh Museum
•p. 94

Rijksmuseum
•p. 90

Stedelijk Museum
•p. 98

Rijksmuseum
•p. 90

**Leidseplein • Vondelpark • Nederlands Filmmuseum •
Concertgebouw • Museumplein • Rijksmuseum •
Van Gogh Museum • Stedelijk Museum • Heineken
Brouwerij •** *The diamonds of Amsterdam*

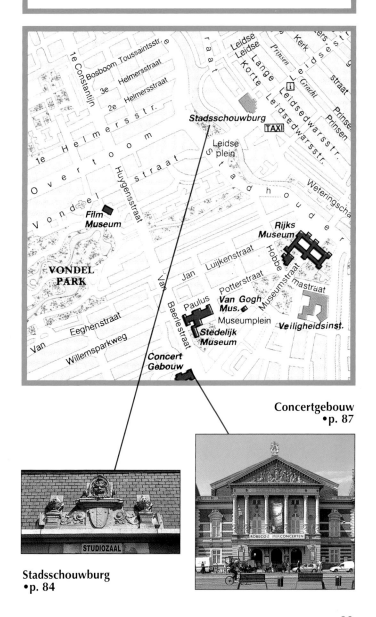

Concertgebouw
• p. 87

Stadsschouwburg
• p. 84

The Stadsschouwburg, the Town Theatre, in busy Leidseplein.

The famous American Hotel built by W. Kromhout in 1897.

LEIDSEPLEIN

It is a window that looks onto the world: you could see it passing in front of you without ever having to move at all. All you have to do is to wait. Cafés, theatres, beer-houses, clubs, all types of meeting-places, legendary pubs, taverns, street shows, mimes, clowns, afro musicians and hard rockers contribute to making Leidseplein the most unrestrained square in Europe. In the centre you will find the **Town Theatre** and the AUB, the information and booking office that covers every show in town. Do not forget a visit of the amazing **American Hotel** next door: W. Kromhout built this hotel in 1897, following the demolition of the previous structure in 1882, in an incredibly beautiful art nouveau style, using architectural elements that were forerunners of the Amsterdam School of Architecture. And do not fail to stop at the *Café Américain*, built in art déco fashion and one of the most elegant meeting places in the city. Everything you see here has an aura of perfection, right down to the tiniest detail, whether it is the candlesticks,

The elegant art déco interior of the Café Américain.

Around Leidseplein – the De Melkweg Theatre, and Paradise, one of the temples of rock music.

the windows, the furnishing or the mosaics. Look around and you'll see imperturbable ladies and gentlemen sipping their tea at the newspaper reading-desk: these will be journalists and writers who have come to read their printed articles in one of Amsterdam's oldest meeting places. In Leidseplein you will find everything imaginable: the **Paradiso**, the deconsecrated church occupied by the provos during the sixties and since then a sanctuary for rock music, and on the other side of the square **De Melkweg**, a large abandoned cheese factory transformed into the home of improvised play-acting and a stage-setting for every young Dutch actor.

VONDELPARK

The statue of Joost van den Vondel, the famous Dutch poet; the park was named after him in 1867.

Part of the Vondelpark, a favourite spot for local citizens.

It is a magnificent park covering over one and a half kilometres and almost 50 hectares wide. Lawns, small lakes, plays of water, a rose-garden and a tea-room create a dreamy atmosphere right in the heart of the city. It is Amsterdam's Bois de Boulogne: on Sundays it is thronged by thousands of city-dwellers in overalls, racing on bicycles or roller-skates, taking the dog for a walk or simply stretching out on the grass. When the park was opened to the public in 1865 it covered about eight hectares of land; nowadays, hundreds of tree and plant species grow here and numerous animals have their habitat.

Right throughout the sixties, during the summer, Vondelpark was the noctural destination of vagant hippies. Their little Saturday market aroused the curiosity of crowds.

Nowadays during the summer months, open air concerts: children's plays and marches of talented music bands are held in Vondelpark.

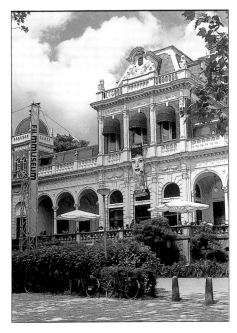

The pavilion that now houses the Nederlands Filmmuseum was designed by the father and son architects called Hamer.

NEDERLANDS FILMMUSEUM

In the pavilion that was opened in 1881 inside the park as a café-restaurant, and which has since undergone renovation several times, we can visit the Nederlands Filmmuseum, which holds an interesting and huge collection of cinematography material as well as a film library.

Over a thousand films are projected every year, and there is also an open-air cinema during the Summer months.

CONCERTGEBOUW

In 1988, for the centenary of the Concertgebouw, the Concert Hall, thorough restoration of this historic place was carried out. The Concertgebouw was built thanks to the pride of six Dutch business-men needled by the ferocious irony of a magazine that accused the inhabitants of Amsterdam of having no knowledge of art because art does not make money. It was laid on thick by Johannes Brahms who, invited to Amsterdam in 1879, did not hesitate to define the Dutch as appalling musicians. This was too much. The six men launched the challenge and in 1883 they supervised the bedding of the first pillars (2,186 in the end) on which the Concertgebouw was to be positioned.

Five years later the building was completed and on the 3rd November 1888 the new National Orchestra gave its first concert under the directorship of Willem Kes. Even though Kes remained director of the Concertgebouw for only seven years, he managed to implant a deep love for music in the Dutch people.

The elegant Neo-Renaissance style Concertgebouw.

His successor, Willem Mengelberg, remained in office for half a century and introduced Mahler and Strauss, succeeding in organising the stirring Mahler Festival.

Very soon the Concertgebouw became one of the most soughtafter destinations of orchestras and composers even if its austere halls also opened their doors to classical music. Great artists such as Louis Armstrong, Count Basie, Lionel Hampton and Frank Sinatra invaded the Concertgebouw where the historic rock concerts of Frank Zappa and The Who were also held.

Conferences, exhibitions, business meetings and political conventions are also held here.

MUSEUMPLEIN

It is much more than a square and not just a tree-lined triangle slightly beyond the historic enclosure of canals. Museumplein is unique in Europe, a square that advanced town planning has turned into an area set aside for museums. Here, in fact, are some of the most important museums in Europe: the Rijksmuseum, a grand labyrinth of huge collections; the vast collection of works by Vincent van Gogh in the museum that bears his name and the modern, fascinating Stedelijk Museum, the Municipal Museum.

RIJKSMUSEUM

The Rijksmuseum is one of the richest museums in the world and most certainly the most complete as far as Dutch art of the Golden Century is concerned. But the collections appear to be endless: the museum has something for everybody. One day is not sufficient for a complete visit, but its real masterpiece which will follow you in every corner of Amsterdam is Rembrandt's "Company of Captain Frans Banning Cocq and Lieutenant Willem van Ruytenburch", better known as *The Night Watch*.

HISTORY – One owes the greatest Dutch museum to a Frenchman. When Napoleonic France took possession of Holland, Louis Bonaparte rose to the throne of The Netherlands which were to be. His decrees included one of the 21st April, 1808 ordering the creation of a large national museum. The king wanted to make Amsterdam one of the most important artistic centres in Europe and decided to arrange this museum in the halls of his residence, that is, in the Royal Palace of the Dam. Louis Bonaparte entrusted the first direc-

The Neo-Gothic façade of the Rijksmuseum.

tor, Johann Meerman de Viren en Delan, with attending to the necessary acquisitions to form a collection worthy of his aspirations. And he certainly did his work properly; the museum opened its doors exhibiting 225 paintings from the National Art Gallery of The Hague and from the Van Pot van Groeneveld collection which was bought for one hundred thousand guilders in Rotterdam. Other important paintings already belonged to the city of Amsterdam and since then, they have been lent to the museum. Amongst these, Rembrandt's masterpiece *The Night Watch* already stood out.

Bonaparte's reign lasted only two years, but the museum was destined to continue: the new king, William I, transferred the collections from the Royal Palace to one of the most luxurious houses in Amsterdam, the Trippenhuis on the Kloveniersburgwal. The museum that was finally called the Rijksmuseum was reopened in 1816. From then onwards donations together with purchases continued at an increasing rate until it was evident that the Trippenhuis could no longer contain such a vast collection.

In 1862 a competition was published for the designing of a new building. 21 architects participated and ten years later, P. J. Cuypers came up with the winning design. On the 13th July, 1885 was the official opening of this spectacular, red brick building in neogothic style, which loomed up beyond the circle of canals, in almost open countryside, right in the very spot where a windmill stood. Right from the very beginning, the Rijksmuseum did not only exhibit collections of paintings, but bought and displayed Asiatic art, collections of objects pertaining to Dutch history and created a Prints Room. For the crowning of Queen Wilhelmina, a large exhibition of Rembrandt's works with special emphasis on *The Night Watch* was organised. As from the Second World War, the Rijksmuseum has carried out continuous research and modernization of its structures, making it one of the most active museums in Europe today.

Rijksmuseum

Moreover, the appearance of the interior is forever changing: in fact, the works of art on view in the picture-gallery are often shifted from one room to another to make space for the numerous temporary exhibitions that are held every now and then in the Rijksmuseum.

Unless the visitor has more than one day to spend seeing the museum, it is practically impossible to look through all 260 of the rooms that hold an incredible amount of works of art, some of which are priceless. It is advisable, therefore, to choose the sections considered most interesting from a personal point of view, selecting them with the aid of the printed plan of the museum that is distributed without charge at the entrance. One part that definitely must not be missed is that on the top floor, where exceptional collections of paintings by 15th-19th century Flemish and Dutch artists can be admired in rooms 201 to 227.

Rembrandt van Rijn: *Self-Portrait.*

Rembrandt van Rijn: *The Board of the Amsterdam Drapers' Guild* (1662).

The room where *The Night Watch*, Rembrandt's most famous painting, is on view.

Rembrandt van Rijn: *The Night Watch* (1642).

Jan Vermeer: *The Milk-maid* (1658).

Rijksmuseum

93

VAN GOGH MUSEUM

Opened in 1973, this modern square building made of plate glass and unfinished concrete, with large halls and vast areas brightly illuminated by daylight, was designed by Gerrit Rietveld to house Van Gogh's work. On view here is the largest and most important collection of his paintings, donated to the city of Amsterdam by the artist's brother, Theo, and by his nephew, Vincent-Willem. This is one of the city's museums that should not be missed. A new wing that has extended the exhibition space considerably, was designed by the Japanese architect, Kisho Kurokawa, and opened in 1999; temporary exhibitions are held here.

The Van Gogh Museum contains 200 of the artist's paintings, about 500 drawings and over 700 of his personal letters. A large collection of paintings and sculptures by other 19th century artists is also on display.

VINCENT VAN GOGH - Van Gogh was born into a family of Protestant clergymen on 30th March 1853, at Zundert in the Brabant province. For a few years he followed in his father's footsteps, studying theology and becoming an assistant minister, but this was not his vocation; he discovered art and took up painting, dedicating the last ten years of his life (four of which were spent in France) completely to it. Van Gogh was affected with a serious form of epilepsy and often suffered hallucinations and episodes of psycho-

Van Gogh Museum – a new elliptic shaped wing built for temporary exhibitions has been added on to the original building that holds permanent exhibitions.

Vincent van Gogh:
The Potato-eaters
(1885).

Vincent van Gogh:
Clogs (1888).

Vincent van Gogh:
Self-Portrait with Felt Hat (1887).

sis; during one these attacks he went as far as cutting off the lobe of one of his ears.

Plagued by his unrelenting illness, he shot himself in the chest on 27th July 1890 while in Auvers-sur-Oise near Paris, the last stop on his wanderings through France; he died two days later.

Interiors - The museum is spread out over four floors, plus a basement that holds an auditorium.

On the ground and third floors there is a huge collection of 19th century paintings and sculptures that all have something in common with Van Gogh's work, some examples of which are amongst them. The first floor holds the artist's most significant paintings. The chronological order of the works on display guides the visitors through the various periods of the artist's life: his first experiences in Nuenen (*The Potato-eaters*, 1885); his stay in Anvers where he studied at the Academy of Fine Arts (portraits and views of the city); his magical period in Paris (17 self-portraits) where his encounter with great artists like Henri de Toulouse-Lautrec, Paul Signac and Georges Seurat introduced him to the latest artistic movements, which he soon adopted, giving the relative techniques his own personal touch and achieving results that turned out to be highly successful; his radiant and productive visit to Arles (*The Yellow House*, 1888; *The Bed-chamber*, 1888; *The Harvest* - probably his best landscape – 1888); then his period of gloom and melancholy – when his illness started to become acute – in Saint-Rémy, where his talent nevertheless produced beautiful paintings (*The Reaper*, 1889; *Almond Blossom*, 1889; *Sunflowers*, 1889; *Still Life with Irises*, 1890); ending up in Auvers-sur-Oise where, in spite of his declining health, he painted his last pieces before committing suicide. Work with an aura of distress and ominous of suicide; paintings that penetrate the soul and on front of which emotions become intense: *Wheatfield under a Cloudy Sky*, and *Wheatfield with Crows*, both dated 1890.

The second floor houses the Hall of Prints, where the various collections of items on paper are rotated and temporarily exhibited. Unfortunately, since exposure to light can cause damage to Van Gogh's letters and drawings, these are only put on view occasionally. This floor also has an area for research, with books and audio-visual equipment available to those who wish to increase their knowledge of 19th century artists.

Vincent van Gogh:
Fishing boats on the Shore at Saintes-Maries-de-la-mer (1888).

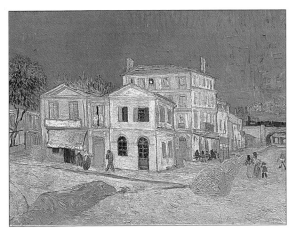

Vincent van Gogh:
The Yellow House
(1888).

Vincent van Gogh:
Harvest (1888).

Vincent van Gogh: *Wheatfield with Crows* (1890).

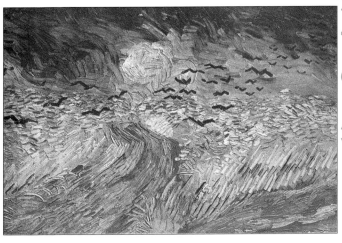

STEDELIJK MUSEUM

It is the municipal museum of the city of Amsterdam and contains one of the most important collections of modern and contemporary art in Europe. Its collections mainly concern the 19th and 20th centuries in The Netherlands and France with their best painters: Cézanne, Monet, Picasso, Matisse, Mondrian, Malevitch, Chagall and Dubuffet.

The red-brick building on the elegant Paulus Potterstraat which houses the Stedelijk Museum was built between 1893 and 1895 by the architect, A. W. Weissman. It is another example of the Dutch Renaissance and its façade is distinguished by numerous niches occupied by statues of Amsterdam's leading artists which inevitably include Hendrick de Keyser and Jacob van Campen. The Stedelijk Museum was built thanks to the generosity of Amsterdam's leading collectionists: the Town Council decided to build the museum when Amsterdam received the collection of Sophia Augusta de Bruyn as a donation in 1891.

Initially the Stedelijk Museum accepted all kinds of collections: the History of Archery, the Museum for measuring time, Oriental art and the museums of the history of medicine. It was only in 1952, when these collections were transferred to more suitable places, that the Stedelijk Museum concentrated only on modern art.

An extension within the museum and the addition of more wings are foreseen to increment the space for permanent and temporary exhibitions.

The Neo-Renaissance exterior of the Stedelijk Museum.

Some of the sculptures are displayed in the museum **gardens** and on front of the new Van Baerlestraat wing. The works of art include items by De Wouters, Moore, Renoir, Laurens, Etienne-Martin, Serra, Visser, Volten, Couzijn, Rodin, Gabo, Pevsner, Duchamp-Villon, Arp, Müller, Richter, Rückriem, Long and Andre, to mention just a few.

Applied art: this collection, which was opened in 1934, consists of handicrafts such as ceramics, furniture, artistic glass, objects in glass and wood.

Prints room: opened in 1956, it includes drawings, prints and water-colours of Dutch and foreign artists. In 1981 photography was also introduced into the Stedelijk collections.

The extremely modern interior of the Stedelijk Museum contrasts with the 19th century exterior of the building.

HEINEKEN BROUWERIJ

The exterior of the Heineken ex-brewery.

A few of the plaques referring to brewing procedures that adorn the walls of the building.

The massive brick building at Stadhouderskade 78, which until 1988 housed the brewery called after Gerard Adriaan Heineken, the man who founded the company in 1864, is now the Heineken Reception Centre.

On weekdays all year round, guided tours take visitors through the ex-brewery and around the stables, where splendid specimens of the breed of horses used to pull the beer wagons are still stabled.

Visitors not only hear of the history of the company but also the procedures entailed in brewing this drink, starting from its discovery many centuries ago. The tour ends with beer tasting, with free tankards for all.

Right: a typical horse-drawn cart for transporting beer.

THE DIAMONDS OF AMSTERDAM

The term diamond is derived from the Greek word "adamas", meaning invincible. Diamonds are the stone encountered in dreams and associated with monarchs, pharaohs and emperors. Formed by carbons in a very pure form which has resisted every kind of geological revolution, they are jewels of unequalled prestige. And Amsterdam is the diamonds' capital.

The first diamond-cutter in Amsterdam was registered over four centuries ago. From then onwards (1584), Amsterdam became synonymous with diamonds for world markets and imperial courts. It all started at the end of the 16th century when merciless religious persecutions broke out. The Spanish drove away the diamond-cutters, who then found refuge in tolerant, liberal Amsterdam. It was only the first step in a long ascent. In 1750 the diamond industry employed 600 persons, but it was only the beginning of its fortune. 1867 was year of the gold rush with the opening of gold diamond mines in South Africa. Amsterdam became the most famous diamond cutting in the world. The Cullinan diamond, which is the largest diamond ever discovered (3106 carats) was cut in Amsterdam into 105 separate stones. The most famous one, known as the "First Star of Africa" forms part of the English Crown Jewels.

In 1936 the first Diamond World Fair was held in Amsterdam. Only 20% of the stones cut in The Netherlands are used as jewels. The remaining 80% are used for other purposes: precision instruments as well as in electronics and in the space and mining industries.

After the slump in trade due to World War II, the diamond industry was able to recover and flourish, and Amsterdam now has many workshops. Many of these are open to visitors, who can watch the various steps of diamond cutting on the spot without being urged to purchase.

Coster Diamonds (Paulus Potterstraat, 2-6), Amsterdam Diamond Center (Rokin, 1-5), Gassan (Nieuwe Uilenburgerstraat, 173-175) and Stoeltie Diamonds (Wagenstraat, 13-17) are just a few of the most prominent workshops.

The 'Amsterdam Cut' trademark is the emblem of maximum precision and perfection throughout the en tire world.

From top to bottom: the Amsterdam Diamond Center, Coster Diamonds and Gassan establishments.

101

**Plantage • Hortus Botanicus • Hollandse Schouwburg •
Artis Zoo • Geological Museum • Planetarium •
Aquarium • *Windmills* • De Gooyer Windmill •
Muiderpoort • Entrepotdok**

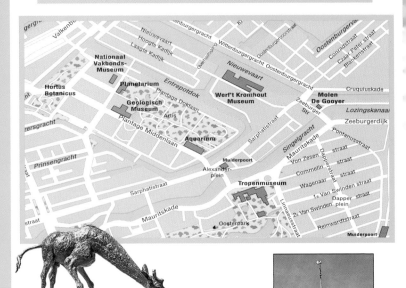

Artis Zoo
•p. 106

Muiderpoort
•p. 110

De Gooyer Windmill
•p. 110

PLANTAGE

If we go down Muiderstraat, which is next to the Portuguese Synagogue, and cross the Nieuwe Herengracht, one of the canals off
the Amstel, we come to the Plantage district.
It's name means 'plantation': quite adapt, too, since this zone to
the East of the city's centre – an area full of vegetation – has been
used by the inhabitants as a place for leisure since the 18th century. Today it is a residential district full of tree-lined avenues, parks
and gardens, but there are also many interesting things to see, such
as the places indicated below. For a long time, the wealthier Jews
of the city inhabited the Plantage and there are numerous monuments still standing that testify their presence.

HORTUS BOTANICUS

The entrance gates to the Botanical Gardens are at Plantage Middenlaan 2A. Its foundation was decided in 1682 and the project
was able to avail of the enormous expansion of the Dutch
colonies. For centuries, both travellers and botanical experts added
collections of plants to the Gardens. Tropical plants brought back
from the East and West Indes were grown here and exported all
over the world.

The entrance to the Botanical Gardens.

For the first time ever outside Arabian territory, even coffee plants were grown here at the beginning of the 19th century. An ordinance from Louis Bonaparte, at that time King of The Netherlands, enriched the Gardens considerably in 1809, and in 1877 the administration was taken over by University of Amsterdam.

Within the Gardens there are two greenhouses which deserve a visit; one, erected in 1913 but recently renovated, contains splendid specimens of palm trees; the other, a more modern structure in plate glass and aluminium, shelters desert plants from tropical and subtropical areas. Today, over two thousand species of trees, exotic flowers, plant varieties and medicinal herbs are grown in the Gardens.

A visit of the Hortus Botanicus is an experience not to be missed because of the great variety of plants grown there and which make it one of the most important in the world.

Right: part of the interior of the butterfly glasshouse.

Hollandse Schouwburg - a pillar erected on a Star of David shaped base, dedicated to deportees, stands in the ex-theatre transformed into a memorial to the Dutch Jews who fell victim to the Nazis.

HOLLANDSE SCHOUWBURG

This is a memorial to the over one hundred thousand Jews who lost their lives during the Second World War. At the time of the war the building was a theatre and sixty thousand Jews were imprisoned in it before being taken to the concentration camps.

Once the war was over the building lay unused until 1961, when it was decided to demolish practically all of it except its façade and foyer; the part previously used for seating spectators became a garden and a tall pillar standing on a base shaped like a Star of David was erected where the stage once stood. The upper floor of the building holds documents and audio-visual media illustrating both the history of the building and the tragic events suffered by the local Jewish community.

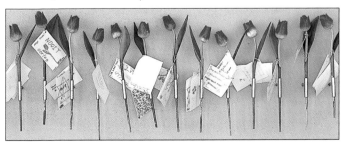

ARTIS ZOO

This large zoological complex was founded in 1838 by Dr. Westerman, chairman of the Natura Artis Magistra (Nature is the teacher of the Arts) association.
At the time it was a place where biologists studied and worked and was not opened to the public until some time after.
The Aquarium, Planetarium and Geological Museum all look out onto the Artis, which is spread out over extensive, well-kept gardens. The enclosures and cages (some rather too small) housing the animals are distributed here and there in the park, amid vegetation, ponds and pathways.
The zoo holds an exceptionally rich selection of mammals, birds, fish, amphibians and reptiles.

GEOLOGICAL MUSEUM

A recently renovated building standing in the south-east corner of the Artis houses this museum; the ticket purchased for visiting the zoo includes entrance to the museum. The section dealing with the evolution of life on Earth is very interesting, as is the large exhibition of fossils and minerals. There are even dinosaurs!

PLANETARIUM

Visitors cannot fail to see the enormous dome that towers over the building immediately to the left of the main entrance.

If one of your hobbies is astronomy, then you'll enjoy the projections shown every hour on a gigantic screen inside the dome; the commentary is in Dutch, but explanations in other languages can be obtained. There is also an interesting display of material concerning astronomy and exploration of outer space, including some models of space ships.

AQUARIUM

The extremely interesting Artis Aquarium is housed in a neo-classic building and was opened in 1882.

In 1997 it was completely renovated and equipped with the latest types of water systems: three provide salt water and one fresh water. The enormous tanks, regulated at different temperatures, contain several hundred species of fish and water animals.

The enormous dome that dominates the Planetarium.

WINDMILLS

In the past, the landscape of the Dutch countryside was characterized by the familiar shapes of windmills, as testified by numerous paintings and prints from the 17th century onwards. The first mills were built in the early part of the Middle Ages for the purpose of exploiting the energy of the wind or water mainly for grinding corn. The windy climate of the Dutch plains favored the diffusion of windmills so much so that they began to be used for various types of activities, before being replaced by electrical motors and combustion engines at the beginning of the industrial revolution. The energy produced by the movement of the blades was used to saw tree trunks, produce linseed-and rape-oil, grind spices for making mustard and manufacture cloth and sails for the ships which plowed the oceans. The contribution of the mills also turned out to be fundamental in snatching new land away from the sea, draining water and reclaiming the big lakes. Today in The Netherlands there are only around 1000 mills left, compared to 9000 in the past. Thanks to the sensitivity of the Dutch population and the intervention of the state, many of these mills have been kept in a working state through maintenance and restoration operations. There are basically two types of mill in Holland: water mills, with wheels operated by the force of water, and windmills which exploit the energy of the wind. Water mills are only found in the eastern and southern provinces of The Netherlands, where rivers and streams with sufficient inclination to make the mill wheels turn are found. Most of these mills are used for grinding cereals. There are, however, many types of windmills, with different forms and functions. The "pillar" windmill is the most ancient type and was already being used in the 13th century. This windmill has a rather distinctive shape: resting on a vertical wooden pillar is the rectangular body of the mill which is free to turn according to the direction of the wind. The cable transmission shaft mill is derived from the "pillar" mill. The rotating body rests on a heavy wooden cylinder inserted into a pyramid-shaped base which is bigger and higher than the former type. Cable transmission shaft mills are very common in southern Holland and the provinces of Utrecht and Brabant, where they are mainly used to drain the polder. "Pasture" windmills are smaller than the others and most common in Northern Holland where they are used as water pumps. The "skirt" windmills of Palatinate are typical of the Zaan region. Their name comes from their distinctive shape, with a projecting roof, reminiscent of a woman's skirt. Today only 4 specimens are left of this type of windmill which were mainly sawmills. Round masonry windmills can be found where there is constant wind power. Usually only the top with the sails turns, following the wind. This type of windmill is very common in Friesland where it is used to drain the polder. Due to their typical shape which brings to mind a cassock, the rounded masonry windmills are popularly called "monks". "Gallery" windmills are found where the mill has to be raised due to the presence of obstacles like trees and tall buildings which block the passage of the wind. These windmills are distinguished by a circular terrace situated at a sufficient height to make it possible to work on the sails. "Elevated" windmills are similar to "gallery" mills but stand on artificial rises instead of being elevated on brickwork. "Tower" windmills, which have a cylindrical stone body, are not very common and their introduction to Holland dates back to the Crusades. Windmills with rotating tops can be found in wood or stone and have hexagonal, octagonal or circular bases. Sometimes it is possible to find windmills arranged in a line. This is necessary when the action of one windmill is not enough to make up the difference between the water level of a polder and that of the surrounding collection canal. To solve this problem, several windmills are placed in a row, each one bringing the water to a certain level, through a system of steps, until the highest part of the collection canal is reached.

A common element in various types of windmills is the internal mechanism which is basically identical. The sails, moved by the force of the wind, are fixed to a transversal shaft which transfers the movement to the mainmast placed perpendicular to the same, through the upper wheel which engages with a pulley on top of the mainmast. At the base of the mast is another system of pulleys and gears which transmit the movement to the various machines located in the base of the windmill. The sails are placed in the direction of the wind so that they can turn with the help of an external rotating system in winch mills, or an internal rotating system in covered mills. The size of the surface area of the sail blades varies according to the speed and intensity of the wind.

Legend

1. Transversal shaft

2. Upper wheel

3. Mainmast

4. Lower wheel

5. Pulley

6. Shaft of the jaw crusher

7. Shaft of the millstone

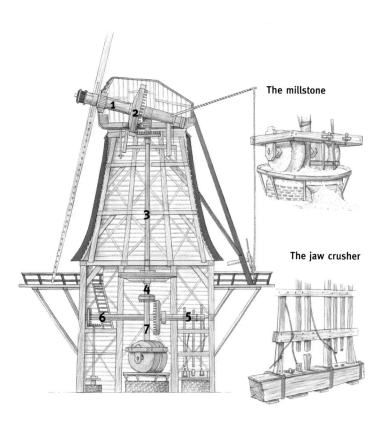

The millstone

The jaw crusher

DE GOOYER WINDMILL

The windmills still standing within the city boundaries can be counted on one hand and the De Gooyer one is that nearest the centre, on Funenkade in the eastern part of the Plantage district. However, this was not its original site: it was built around 1725 slightly farther to the South then, almost a hundred years after, because of the presence of military barracks hindering the wind passing through the vanes, it was dismantled bit by bit and reassembled on its present site in Funenkade. It was a windmill for grinding wheat and its aerodynamic vanes were very modern for its time. During the 1920's, when the windmill was starting to fall to pieces, the local municipal authorities bought it and restored it completely. Nearby, at no. 7 of the same street, there is a small brewery that offers beer tasting inside the windmill itself.

MUIDERPOORT

This is the gateway that Napoleon passed through when entering the city in 1811; it stands on the Alexanderplein, in the north-eastern part of the Plantage district. In 1770, Cornelius Rauws restructured considerably what was originally erected at the beginning of the 18th century. A dome bearing a clock tower surmounts the gateway, and the emblem of Amsterdam can be seen on the gate façade.

The De Gooyer Windmill – one of few windmills left standing within the city boundaries.

Muiderpoort – the gateway through which Napoleon entered Amsterdam in 1811.

ENTREPOTDOK

Around the end of the 1980's, the over eighty warehouses in the half kilometre-long row bordering this canal underwent substantial transformation. These buildings had been erected between 1708 and 1829 for storing trading goods belonging to the VOC, the Dutch East Indes Company, and until halfway through the 19th century this storage area was the largest in Europe.

Nowadays, it is the site of exclusive offices, cafés, restaurants and dwellings!

Some of the buildings still have the original warehouse façades, while their interiors have been completely transformed and even small courtyards have been created.

The tables of the cafés and restaurants bordering the canal overlook the brightly painted houseboats moored to the wharves.

Entrepotdok – the old warehouses that have been restored and converted into exclusive residences and offices.

THE CANALS

In order to have an overview of Amsterdam it is necessary to fly over it, which is quite possible during the summer as air trips over the city are organised, or to have a map of its central area constantly on hand. Only in this way is it possible to appreciate it and understand why this extraordinary network of canals have made the Dutch capital be rebaptized as the Venice of the North.

The best approach to Amsterdam and the best way to appreciate how this city was founded and has developed is a boat trip down the canals. Amsterdam is a semicircle, a half moon which extends from its natural centre, the artificial island with its Central Station, towards the countryside and the land which has been protected over the centuries from recurring floods. A trip in a pleasure boat enables one to discover that Amsterdam

Both pages: some of the typical houseboats on the canals and, top right, the barge belonging to pacifists moored on the Singel.

is not an imperial city built by pretentious, ambitious sovereigns. Amsterdam is a city whose houses and buildings were erected by rich middle-class, enlightened lovers of beauty with exquisite taste and a passion for details and refinement. Amsterdam is a city of merchants and tradesmen, but it is also a city lacking in superfluous ostentation. Here capitalism took its first steps and underwent its initial tests. It was an almost perfect form of capitalism, full of common sense and tolerance, to the extent that its lack of defects made it almost boring. But the end result was that it gave us an extraordinary, privileged, tidy city, whose canals are a faithful, fascinating mirror. The rings of canals were a miracle of town-planning in Amsterdam and are the work of a great architect, Staets, and a burgomaster, Oetgens. They had to manage and direct plan and program the first great expansion of the city beyond the fortified walls which protected it along that belt which was destined to become the innermost canal, the **Singelgracht**. This was at the beginning of the Golden Century, but the greatness and strength of Amsterdam were already manifest. The city burst out from its walls and sprawled beyond the Singelgracht.

This was in 1613 and Amsterdam was in keeping with its commercial power. It took some ten years to urbanize its outermost area, **Prinsengracht** and **Lijnbaansgracht**. The architects of the Golden Century built magnificent houses along the canals; they had a preference for bell-shaped or circle

façades with flights of steps, whereas architects of the 18th century initiated stone balustrades and red-brick façades.

The canals were also destined to rewrite Amsterdam's social history, redrawing up the map of the districts and places where people wanted to live. It was a pursuit of beauty, enrichment and prestige. The richest and most elegant people chose the **Herengracht**, the Gentlemen's canal, with it refined baroque façades. Socialites built their lavish homes on the **Keizersgracht**, the Emperor's canal. Those who lived on the Singelgracht or the outermost canal, the Prinsengracht, had no time for farces. They were the merchants of all merchants and the most popular amongst the nouveaux riches; their houses reflected their franctic activities.

Nowadays the canals are one of Amsterdam' most extraordinary monumental aspects. 75 thousand trees shade these town rivers, 7000 houses are declared national monuments and 1000 bridges join banks and islands. There are 85 kilometres of water regulated by a complex system of sluices which control their flow. They are also a way of communicating: for example the refuse disposal service use large, slow-moving barges to collect garbage. But they are also dwelling places and thousands of **house-boats** can be seen along the canals. The last census recorded over two thousand, almost half of which were without licenses and moored in double or triple rows with no intention of setting sail again. Originally used as make-shift homes after the German bombings in 1940, they have become part and parcel of the landscape. Sumptuously decorated with flowers, plants and trees and with lively designs and embroidered curtains, some are luxury models wheareas others are occupied by young communities. Others are real bath-tubs. They all provide an answer to Amsterdam's most important sights along the canals. Special trips are organised: a three and a half hour trip and a night cruise by candle light. The largest companies and the docking wharves are around the station on the Damrak. Others are behind Leidseplein or on the Rokin, near Muntplein. In recent years, the "De Grachtenfiets", the habit of renting an authentic pedal boat to travel around the canals and disturb the peace of inhabitants of the house-boats, has become common practice.

SINGELGRACHT

It is Amsterdam's innermost canal, the narrowest circle of the half-moon of canals. Its name means ring or belt and it marked the boundary of the medieval town, the first Amsterdam which was built around the Dam and developed in the direction of Walletjes. Before the 17th century, the Singelgracht was merely a ditch separating the town walls, which rose on the side of the odd numbers, from the gardens and lawns of Amsterdam's immediate outskirts. When the town passed the ditch, the walls no longer had any reason for being there and houses sprung up along the banks of the Singelgracht. One of the town's most quaint houses was built at **no. 7**: the narrowest in absolute terms, no wider than a door. An authentic record and clever trick to avoid excessive taxes. In fact, in Amsterdam taxes on houses were paid according to the space that they occupied along the canals or streets; that is why all owners tried to build upwards instead of sidewards. At **nos. 19-21** stands a special house, whose central part was transformed into a warehouse in 1760. At **nos. 66-68** are two twin 18th-century houses. There are another two twin houses at **nos. 104-106** with their gables sumptuously decorated. At **nos. 140-142** is a house designed by Hendrick de Keyser, one of the most famous architects in Amsterdam. Between 1605 and 1655 it was the residence of a captain of the municipal police, Frans Banning Cocq, destined to become famous

Singelgracht – the narrowest house in Amsterdam at no. 7 and the twin houses at nos. 104-106.

Singelgracht – top, centre left and bottom left: the house designed by Hendrick de Keyser at nos. 140-142. Below right: the house at no. 423 built in 1606.

because he was immortalized by Rembrandt as the leader of his company of militiamen in the great Dutch painter's most famous painting *The Night Watch.* Lastly, along the Singelgracht lies the **University** (see page 44) and, in its final section, before Muntplein, the floating **Flower Market** (see page 71).

Herengracht – top left to right: at nos. 43-45, two of the typical warehouses that have been renovated; the Theatre Museum at no. 168 and the Bartolotti House next door. Below: the Van Brienenhuis at no. 284 and the house at no. 314.

HERENGRACHT

It was the residential canal, the Gentlemen's canal, modelled after 1612 when the city grew non-stop. The richest, most enlightened merchants came to live along this canal, competing with one another as to who had the most beautiful and largest house. It is the canal with the most impressive façades, soughtafter coats-of-arms and imposing pediments. Over 400 houses on the Herengracht are considered national monuments. They are mainly occupied by offices and banks as their maintenance is too expensive for private ownership. The Herengracht connects the Amstel to the south east with the Brouwersgracht to the north.

At **nos. 43-45** two recently restored warehouses are considered the oldest constructions on the canal. At **no. 115** is a house erected by

Herengracht – between nos. 338 and 370, more of the elegant buildings facing the canal.
Centre: the house at no. 475 and, below, the one at no. 527 where Tsar Peter the Great was once one of the guests.

the famous architect, H. P. Berlage. The Neo-classic building at no168 is known as the **White House** because of its sandstone façade designed by Vingboons in 1638. At present it is the site of the **Theatre Museum**, one of the wings of which is in the nearby **Bartolotti House**, at nos. 170-172. Hendrick de Keyser built it in red bricks in 1622 for a brewer, Willem van den Heuvel, who not only brewed beer but also went as far as becoming the owner of the Bartolotti Bank, even taking on its name.

At no. 284, the **Van Brienenhuis** is occupied by the Hendrick de Keyser Foundation. It was built in 1720 for a French Huguenot, Frédéric Blanchard. The Van Brienen family donated it in 1933 after it had been abandoned for almost a hundred years to the foundation whose purpose is to salvage buildings in Amsterdam.

At **no. 314** is to be found a 1720 house which belonged to Nicolas Roswinckel who was also mayor of Moscow. Between **nos. 338** and **370** one can admire some of the most beautiful houses of the Herengracht built between the mid-17th century and 1725. At no. 366 is the **Bible Museum**.

The most beautiful house on the canal is located at **no. 475**. It was built between 1668 and 1672 by a stone-rich merchant, Denys Nuyst and is a compact building with five windows per storey. In 1731 the widow of a fabrics merchant, Petronella van Lennep de Neufville, made important changes to the house. She had the façade decorated by Daniel Marot, while Ignatius van Logterens sculptured two female figures on the sides of the main window. At **no. 502** stands a large house built in 1679 for a merchant, Paul Godin. Since 1927 it has been the official residence of the mayor of Amsterdam. The house at **no. 527** dates back to 1667 and has an unusual history. The Tsar, Peter the Great, stayed there during his long visit to Holland. He left the house in such a bad state that its owner prefered to sell it rather than repair it. But it was not the end of illustrious guests: in 1808, the King Louis Bonaparte stayed here before moving to the Royal Palace in Dam square.

To end the long trip down the Herengracht, at no. 605 is another magnificent house, the **Willet-Holthuysen Museum** (see page 77), a perfect example of an upper middle class residence of the 19th century.

KEIZERSGRACHT

The Emperor's canal owes its name to Maximilian I, ruler of the Holy Roman Empire. The Keizersgracht connects the Amstel, in line with the famous wooden drawbridge – the **Magere Brug** (see page 76) – to the Brouwersgracht. Its houses are not as imposing as those of the parallel Herengracht, but they still keep their charm with some very valuable treasures. The most interesting strip of the canal lies between Westermarkt, Westerkerk square, and Vijzelstraat. During the 19th century, it was tradition after the Sunday church service to promenade in one's Sunday best along this part of the canal.

At no. 123 one can admire one of Amsterdam's most famous houses: the "Huis met de Hoofden", or **House of the Heads**. Built in 1622 by Pieter de Keyser, the House of the Heads is a classic example of Dutch Renaissance architecture. In 1643 it was the residence of the "iron king", Louis de Geer, the stone-rich owner of vast mineral deposits in Sweden. Its gable is decorated with six classical busts. Rumour has it that there was a seventh female bust and legend has it that a rich merchant's servants included a deaf maid. One day when the maid was alone at home, thieves tried to break in, but this deaf servant drove them away. The six busts of the gable are said to represent the unfortunate burglars.

Keizersgracht – an example of Dutch Renaissance style, the House of Heads at no. 123 is considered one of the most beautiful houses in Amsterdam.

At **no. 546** is a lovely house with a bell-shaped gable in Louis XV style. At **no. 672** is yet another famous house built in 1671 according to a plan by

The Van Loon Museum at Keizersgracht no. 672.

Adriaan Dortsman: a classic façade crowned by a stone balustrade. The first owner of this house was the artist Ferdinand Bol and it then passed through the hands of some of the most influential families of Amsterdam: the Trips, the Bas, the Van Hagens and the La Fargues. All families of rich merchants and art-lovers. In 1884 it was bought by the Van Loon family. Since 1973, it has housed the **Van Loon Museum**.

PRINSENGRACHT

It is the most popular of Amsterdam's main canals and the outermost ring of its semicircumference. In fact, the Prinsengracht or Princes' canal marks the outer boundary of the centre of Amsterdam. For a long strip, it skirts the Jordaan, the city's most charming district. At no. 36 is a 1650 house in Dutch Renaissance style with a coat-of-arms representing a sleeping bag: **De Veersack**. Facing it on the opposite bank are a series of **old warehouses**, from no. 187 to no. 217.
The **house of Anne Frank**, transformed into a museum is to be found at no. 263 (see page 20). Next to it looms the bell-tower of the Westerkerk, one of Amsterdam's symbols (see page 19).
At no. 436 Prinsengracht is one of Amsterdam's **Courts of Justice**.

THE PORT

An excursion along the canals usually ends with a quick trip around Amsterdam's gigantic port. It is one of the world's leading ports, even though it suffers from century-old rivalry with Rotterdam. Amsterdam has overcome enormous difficulties with the port that is 19 kilometres away from the open sea.

Until the 17th century, large Dutch merchant vessels used to reach the North Sea by sailing through the wide arms of the Zuidersee. The progressive silting up of this vast bay complicated navigation until it risked blocking it. In 1818 a remedy was found by digging the **Dutch Channel**. But soon this channel proved to be insufficient for the requirements of the large port of Amsterdam. Therefore a direct channel between the centre of the port and the North Sea was engineered. Work on the **North Sea Channel** commenced in 1872; 18 km long, it was completed four years later. At the time it was one of the greatest water works ever constructed. Amsterdam was then once again ready to compete with Rotterdam and reopened its quays to commercial traffic.

Havengebouw – there is a magnificent panorama from the top of this tower at the port.

Prinsengracht – this large Neo-classic building has been the Courts of Justice since 1829. Before that it was an orphanage.

Views of Amsterdam port.

The port of Amsterdam and its seaward channel are two huge basins protected against the tides; large shops docking in Amsterdam do not have to resort to harbour tugs. The whole harbour area has been reclaimed from the sea and its quays for a total length of 40 km are built on artificial islands. Amsterdam's Central Station which is also built on an artificial island, is the point of contact between the western and eastern areas of the harbour. Next to it looms the **Havengebouw**, a 13-storey building built in 1960 by the architect Dudok and housing the harbour administration offices. From a restaurant on the top floor of this skyscraper, one has an excellent view of the harbour. Every year this port receives over 6500 ships for an overall traffic of twenty million tons of goods.

Werf 't Kromhout Museum – this old shipyard now holds a small museum dedicated to the history of naval engineering and of the shipyard itself.

WERF 'T KROMHOUT MUSEUM

The shipyard that houses this small museum started its activity half way through the 18th century. As time passed there was a demand for increasingly large vessels, and the yards gradually underwent reorganisation. Nowadays it is used for refitting boats. The museum, which holds a good sized collection of the engines of boats built in the Kromhout shipyards, is particularly and probably solely appreciated by experts and by people interested in naval engineering.

NEDERLANDS SCHEEPVAART MUSEUM

This is one of the most important naval museums in existence and traces the glorious history of Dutch navigation from the 17th century to this day. The imposing, three-storey building that houses it in Kattenburgerplein no. 1 was designed by Daniël Stalpaert and its construction finished in 1656. Until 1973 it was the headquarters of the Admiralty of The Netherlands, then it became this museum in 1981.

Atlases, prints, nautical charts, globes, naval instruments and equipment, paintings, figureheads, plus a collection of 500 models of ships and boats, offer visitors a vast panorama of both the Military and the Merchant Navy in The Netherlands, as well as its fishing industry. William the First's elegant royal barge, built in 1818, and the Blaeu atlas, printed in Amsterdam in 1663, are but two of the many interesting items on view.

The Netherlands Maritime Museum – the main entrance and views of the inner courtyard.

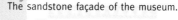

The sandstone façade of the museum.

The *Amsterdam* moored on the banks of the Oosterdok is a true scale reproduction of the *Batavia*, which sunk off the Australian shores in 1629.

Moored outside lies the *Amsterdam*, a model built to true scale of the triple-masted *Batavia*, a sailing ship belonging to the East Indiaman class and once flying the VOC flag. On board, people in traditional costume re-enact scenes of the crew's daily life.

AMSTERDAM
CITY
OF
MUSEUMS

The museums in Amsterdam are normally open from 10 a.m. to 5 p.m. during weekdays and from 1 p.m. to 5 p.m. on Sundays. They are usually closed on Mondays and are always closed on religious and national holidays. Before planning visits it is advisable to enquire at the AUB (Amsterdams Uitburo) in Leidseplein, on the corner of Marnixstraat; their offices are open every day from 10 a.m. to 6 p.m., and to 9 p.m. on Thursdays. Information and bookings may be obtained by telephoning them between 9 a.m. and 9 p.m. every day.
Below is a list of the city's main museums, collections and monuments.

ALLARD PIERSON MUSEUM
127 Oude Turfmarkt
See page 45

AMSTELKRING MUSEUM
("Ons' lieve Heer op solder")
40 Oudezijds Voorburgwal
See page 36

AMSTERDAMS HISTORISCH
MUSEUM
92 Kalverstraat
See page 64

ANNE FRANKHUIS
263 Prinsengracht
See page 20

DE APPEL STICHTING
263 Nieuwe Spiegelstraat
Centre of Contemporary art.

AQUARIUM
40 Plantage Kerklaan
See page 107

ARCAM – Amsterdam
213 Waterlooplein
Centre for architecture.

ARTIS AMSTERDAM ZOO
38-40 Plantage Kerklaan
See page 106

BEURS VAN BERLAGE
MUSEUM
1 Beursplein
See page 31

BIJBELS MUSEUM
366-368 Heerengracht
Objects of biblical archaeology.

GEOLOGISCH MUSEUM
38-40 Plantage Kerklaan
See page 106

HASH MARIHUANA
MUSEUM
148 Oudezijds Achterburgwal
The 80-century-old history of the cannabis.

HOLLANDSE SCHOUWBURG
24 Plantage Middenlaan
See page 105

HORTUS BOTANICUS
2A Plantage Middenlaan
See page 103

JOODS HISTORISCH
MUSEUM
2-4 Jonas Daniël Meijerplein
See page 61

KIT TROPENMUSEUM
2 Linnaeustraat
Exhibitions about the daily life of people of the Tropics.

KONINKLIJK PALEIS
Dam
See page 12

MADAME TUSSAUD SCENERAMA
20 Dam - above the Peek & Cloppenburg department store.
See page 15

NATIONAAL LUCHTVAARTMUSEUM AVIODOME
201 Westelijke Randweg, Schiphol airport
History of aviation and space flights.

NEDERLANDS FILMMUSEUM
3 Vondelpark
See page 87

NEDERLANDS SCHEEPVAART MUSEUM
1 Kattenburgerplein
See page 124

PLANETARIUM
40 Plantage Kerklaan
See page 107

PETER STUYVESANT STICHTING
21 Drentestraat
Exhibition of paintings and modern sculpture.

REMBRANDTHUIS, MUSEUM HET
4-6 Jodenbreestraat
See page 54

RIJKSMUSEUM
42 Stadhouderskade
See page 90

SEXEMUSEUM
26 Damrak
Museum of sex.

STEDELIJK MUSEUM
13 Paulus Potterstraat
See page 98

THEATERMUSEUM
168 Herengracht
See page 118
Dutch theatre history.

UNIVERSITEITSMUSEUM (De Agnietenkapel)
231 Oudezijds Voorburgwal
History of Amsterdam University and student's life. It is housed in a Gothic chapel of 1470.

VAN GOGH MUSEUM
7 Paulus Potterstraat
See page 94

VAN LOON MUSEUM
672 Keizersgracht
Family's private collection on show in the elegant 17th century-house.

WERF 'T KROMHOUT MUSEUM
147 Hoogte Kadijk
See page 123

WILLET-HOLTHUYSEN MUSEUM
605 Herengracht
See page 77

INDEX